THE
CONSERVATORY
month-by-month

THE
CONSERVATORY

month-by-month

BARBARA ABBS

David & Charles

Photographs by Neil Campbell-Sharp pp2, 54, 120;
Garden Picture Library pp6 (John Miller), 20 (John Glover), 32 (Ron Sutherland), 86
(Steven Wooster), 96 (Marie O'Hara), 108 (Mayer/LeScanff), 130 (Lynne Brotchie);
Harpur Garden Library p66; S.& O. Mathews pp3, 8, 10, 44, 74

A DAVID & CHARLES BOOK

Book design by Diana Knapp

Colour and black and white artwork by Michael Lye and Eva Melhuish

First published in the UK in 1997

A catalogue record for this book is available from the British Library.

ISBN 0 7153 0493 3

Typeset by ABM Typographics Ltd, Hull
and printed in Italy by New Interlitho SpA
for David & Charles
Brunel House   Newton Abbot   Devon

CONTENTS

INTRODUCTION

 My first conservatory came with the house and had seen better days. Round it were heavy cast-iron pipes, going nowhere and covered with an elaborate wrought-iron grille; it was roofed with corrugated plastic, punctured with large holes. Wooden slatted shelves down one side held a dusty collection of cacti and two or three very leggy geraniums. It faced into the sun and prevailing wind and was hot and dry in the summer, cold, draughty and damp all winter.

The experience of this conservatory taught me that almost nothing grows successfully in conditions that are the reverse of what they should be. I bought several expensive exotic plants and watched them succumb to the winter damp or the scorching summer sun. Gardening outside seemed infinitely more rewarding, and the conservatory was relegated to growing seeds. Then the plastic roof was replaced with watertight glass and I started again. After two or three years I had created a dense jungle of plumbago, passion flowers, vines and *Mirabilis jalapa* that refused to be outdone and grew to 1¹/₂m (5ft) high, with leaves the size of spinach beet. Despite the fact that nothing flowered very well because most of the light had been excluded, I was so grateful my plants grew at all that I did not dare to prune them.

I know my experience is not unique. Too many garden rooms and conservatories, built with such high hopes, become repositories of badly grown pelargoniums, or a home for bicycles, wellington boots and seed trays. Yet with a number of carefully chosen specimens and a minimum of main-

The pale colours of the flowers and the contrasts of foliage in this conservatory create an atmosphere that is cool and enticing in the summer and in winter the white walls reflect the light. The simple reed blinds and climbing plants trained across the windows and over the roof filter the bright sunlight in summer

tenance, they could be floral drawing rooms, giving pleasure all year round: whatever the aspect, there are plants that will flourish.

Newcomers to conservatory gardening should start modestly. Do not buy large tender plants until you know what temperature you can comfortably sustain in the conservatory during the winter. If your conservatory faces the sun, large-leaved evergreens will not enjoy temperatures which could well be over 32°C (90°F) in the summer. It is very discouraging to watch beautiful and expensive plants die. I know. I have presided over the death beds of oleanders, bouganvilleas, citrus, tibouchina, hibiscus, and many others. If I still had every plant I had ever bought, I would need the temperate house at Kew to contain them. One or two plants, however, have been utterly reliable year after year, through plastic and through glass, for nearly two decades. One is *Hoya carnosa*, the Australian wax flower, which is hardier than is generally believed, at least with me: it has survived temperatures of below freezing. It never needs pruning and scarcely ever repotting. The other, also a climber, is *Campsis radicans*, a deciduous climber which is almost hardy out-of-doors, but flowers earlier and more reliably under glass. Succeeding with these, encouraged me to continue conservatory gardening. I have learnt not to scorn plants which will survive outside. This applies particularly to those that flower in winter. How much time do you spend looking at your snowdrops, bergenia, early daffodils, even camellias and azaleas in the garden during winter? In a conservatory you can enjoy their unspoilt flowers every day they are in bloom. It is far more satisfying than the reproachful appearance of a flowerless and attenuated Chilean glory flower (*Tibouchina urvilleana*).

On the other hand, do not be afraid to experiment. Many conservatory plants are

now widely available as 'patio plants' and are surprisingly inexpensive. Pot plants and 'dot' plants are often very cheap and can be grown on to make majestic specimens. Many 'tender' plants are hardier than they are reputed to be, especially if kept dry during the winter; others are simply so beautiful that if they die after one flowering season, it will have been worth it for those moments of glory. Like arias in an opera, you regret their passing but providing there is enough in the way of scenery and recitative, the show will go on. For a conservatory is an illusion; it is a theatre, and you are the director. What play you choose is entirely up to you. It can be as elaborate as you like, with a cast of thousands or confined to one or two major players. The set can be exuberant or minimal, it can be exotic, nostalgic or dramatically modern; you can create a tropical rainforest or a desert.

The size and aspect of the conservatory determines which plants will contribute to the effect you want. But even the most unpromising can be the stage for something. A draughty conservatory could shelter a collection of alpines; a shady one can be home to a group of ferns. Even a scorchingly hot conservatory has its merits: grow an olive tree and some zonal pelargoniums and create a sun-baked mediterranean terrace.

Whatever you do, do not waste your conservatory. It is a wonderful opportunity to be creative and in touch with nature all year round.

HOW TO USE THIS BOOK

Each chapter is devoted to a month in the conservatory. The tasks of the month may look daunting but you do not have to do them all. Many are for the enthusiastic gardener and are concerned with propagating various species. Essential tasks, which it is important to find time for, are those concerned with heating, ventilation, shading and watering. Next, deal with feeding and pest control. Then do any necessary potting, repotting and pruning.

There is a good selection of plants suitable for conservatory cultivation. They are labelled Easy, Challenging, Cool and shady, and Fragrant; of course, there is a lot of overlap: some of the easy plants are fragrant and

SEASONS

SPRING	AUTUMN
Early: March	Early: September
Mid: April	Mid: October
Late: May	Late: November

SUMMER	WINTER
Early: June	Early: December
Mid: July	Mid: January
Late: August	Late: February

the fragrant plants can be challenging. Cool and shady plants are not necessarily the hardiest; they are plants that prefer coolness in summer and dislike direct sun. They will flourish in a north-facing conservatory but may still need good light. The hardiness of all plants varies from clone to clone, even within a variety. Minimum temperatures are given for most plants, but they will often surprise you by surviving lower ones.

Although the book is divided into months, flowering times vary according to the conditions inside the conservatory and the weather outside. Unless the conservatory is heated to a specific temperature and provided with artificial light, in a cold, dull winter, many plants will flower later than they will in a mild one.

The projects are designed to help you improve your conservatory – its appearance and the conditions within it. You do not have to do them all in one year. Only you can judge what is needed and how much time you can devote to the task.

Two helpful things to remember which will save a lot of heartache:

More plants die from overwatering than underwatering

Pests can often be dealt with manually if spotted early enough

The marmalade bush, Streptosolen jamesonii, *comes from Colombia. In spring it is covered with clusters of these small, bright orange flowers. It has a loose, scrambling habit which allows it to be trained very effectively against a wall, as you would a climber*

J A N U A R Y

*A conservatory is a perfect remedy for the gloomy days of midwinter.
Even in an unheated one there is much to see. If your conservatory is
not quite the show piece it could be, now is the time to plan a flowering
programme for the year.*

*Several Australian plants are in full bloom, particularly the delicately
scented clusters of sharpest yellow on the acacias but also the rosy
hanging bells of* Correa 'Mannii' *and the fragrant brown* Boronia.
*These all do well in the coolish conditions that suit camellias.
Azaleas are still a colourful feature and tone richly with the jewel-like
shades of cinerarias or the paler and more delicate cyclamen and*
Primula obconica. *Most of the daphne family are hardy enough to
flourish out-of-doors but under glass their wonderful perfume can be
fully appreciated. If you have a daphne growing outside, take a cutting
from it in summer, pot it up and soon you will be able to enjoy the
unique daphne scent for three months, from midwinter right through to
early spring.*

*The old adage 'When the days begin to lengthen, then the cold begins to
strengthen' is a good motto to remember throughout this month. The
coldest weather is probably yet to come and freezing temperatures now
are more likely to last for several days at a time. Many good
conservatory plants can stand a degree or so of frost for a short
period but may succumb to a prolonged cold spell. The conservatory
owner needs to be prepared.*

*If your conservatory seems to be lacking colour, particularly in the
early part of the month, take the opportunity to move flowering
houseplants, azaleas, cyclamen, poinsettias and even forced hyacinths
and narcissi, out into it. They will appreciate the moister, cooler air
and flower for much longer. Don't be tempted to add African violets to
this list: they will not enjoy the fluctuating temperatures.*

tasks

FOR THE

month

CHECKLIST

- Keep plants warm
- Force shrubs
- Forced bulbs
- Water provision

SOWING SEEDS
If you have a propagator or heated bench (see p.136), you can start sowing seeds of begonia, pelargonium, streptocarpus, impatiens, lobelia, and calceolaria at the end of the month.

LACHENALIAS (p.10)
Lachenalia aloides var. quadricolor has a long flowering season. See p.88 for planting details

KEEP PLANTS WARM

If you do not have a maximum and minimum thermometer, make it a priority purchase and go out and buy one; best of all, buy two, one for outside and one for inside. Use them to discover the microclimates in the conservatory and the difference between the temperature outside and in. You will probably find that there are several degrees difference between the area near the house wall and any connecting door, and the conservatory windows. If you have an unheated conservatory, but one that is sheltered from cold winds by house walls and gets the sun, this will probably have a temperature range approximating that described in books on greenhouses, as 'Cool greenhouse' with a minimum of 4°C (39°F).

If the conservatory is not heated by a separately controlled section of your house central-heating system, the easiest way of ensuring the survival of plants during cold snaps is to use a thermostatically controlled electric fan heater. These are expensive to run, but easy to use. In addition, it has been proved that the plants benefit enormously from the movement of air that a fan heater creates. The temperature does not need to be set too high, 5°C (41°F) will do the trick. If this is out of the question, tender plants that require slightly higher temperatures will need to be kept as near to the house wall as possible, benefiting from the warmth it has absorbed from light during the day. Only leave extremely hardy plants near the windows if frost is forecast. Even these will benefit from a covering of horticultural fleece on cold nights.

Plants can also be grouped on a heated propagating bench and covered with bubble polythene overnight. (See also Making a heated propagator p.136.) Double polycarbonate walled cloches have also been found to work very well, either on a heated bench or just on the floor. This is particularly effective for fuchsias and pelargoniums.

Alternatively, you can wrap up plants more permanently as is sometimes done in the garden. Pack them around with straw, bracken, or newspaper, and keep this in place with sacking, fleece or bubble polythene tied round it. This does, however, detract from the ornamental appearance of the conservatory when plants like azaleas, acacias, camellias

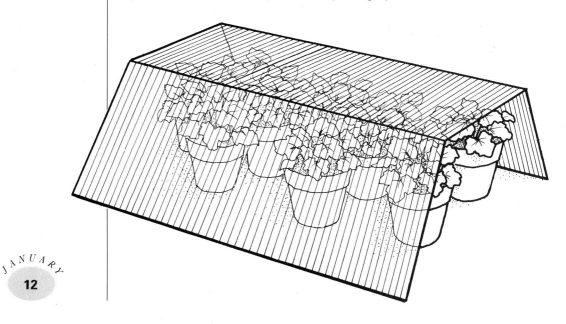

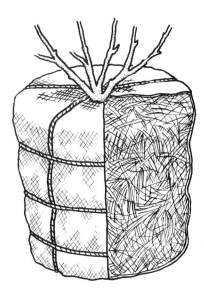

and the earliest spring bulbs will be at their best.

If the conservatory is very exposed, with glass to the ground, don't forget the possibilities of the spare bedroom or a dry cellar. These are safe places to overwinter tender plants. William Robinson in 1867 was very impressed with the way the Paris Parks Department kept all their tender plants in cellars from October to May: lantanas, brugmansias and other exotics were kept dry and dark for many months, and brought out as soon as temperatures were suitable.

FORCING SHRUBS

Lilacs, roses, hydrangeas, deutzias, philadelphus, forsythias and flowering currants can all be forced into flower early to decorate the conservatory. The exquisitely delicate flowers of a shrub like *Syringa* x *josiflexa* 'Bellicent', normally only noticed as decorative clusters on a large bush, can really be appreciated at close quarters. They need to be

either pot-grown or established in large pots (23–30cm/9–12in) in JI No. 2 for about a year before being brought into the conservatory in midwinter. Keep them at a temperature of about 10°C (50°F). Spray daily with tepid water and keep well-watered, especially when flowering. Use a good liquid feed every ten days. Shrubs should be forced like this only every other year and should be stood outside as soon as they have finished flowering. Do not forget to feed and water them regularly.

NOTE

■ *Garden centres often sell deciduous shrubs very cheaply in winter. Make regular visits to your local nursery or garden centre throughout the year to look for bargains. It makes an inexpensive way of experimenting with 'forcing' and stocking the conservatory for the winter months* ■

FORCED BULBS

Miniature irises, ornithogalums, snowdrops planted and left outside eight weeks ago, can be brought into the conservatory now if the shoots are about 2.5cm (1in) high. They will come into flower quickly. (Leave crocuses and muscari outside until next month.) Examine pots carefully for snails, slugs and woodlice beforehand.

WATERING

Many plants, such as citrus, correas, leptospermums, azaleas and camellias need soft water. If you get this from an outside water-butt, fill a watering can and let it stand in the conservatory for some hours before using it so that the water temperature is similar to that in the conservatory. Tap water too will benefit from being warmed up a little during the coldest months. Try not to splash water on flowers, leaves or floor.

Water plants sparingly once a week at most. Once a fortnight may be sufficient. If in doubt, test the compost by pressing your thumb well down into it. If it feels damp, do not water.

ROUTINE TASKS

If the temperature is not below 4°C (39°F), you can still ventilate the conservatory on a sunny dry day

If the day is bright, making the temperature inside the conservatory rise, but it is still near freezing outside, open the door or doors into the house to provide a movement of air

Inspect plants regularly for whitefly, powdery mildew or botrytis. Take remedial action if any of these are present. (See p.47)

Pick off and destroy all dead, rotting or wilted leaves

If you potted up some wallflowers and stocks from the late spring sowing, these can be brought indoors now to flower early

Potted up strawberry runners from autumn can be brought into an unheated conservatory now (see Forcing Strawberries p.104)

Young peach, nectarine and apricot trees can be planted (see p.105)

Citrus trees will be in flower this month. Watch out for scale insects (see p.103)

Flowering plants such as cyclamens, primulas, cinerarias and heathers can be moved into the conservatory and put in full light at 13–16°C (55–61°F). Water carefully

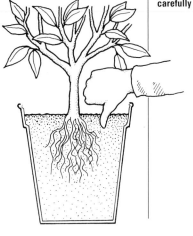

plants
OF THE
month
1

▼
DAPHNE
(Daphne odora 'Aureo-marginata'*)*

All the daphnes are sweetly scented and early flowering. *D. odora* 'Aureo-marginata' has the added advantage of evergreen leaves lightly margined with gold. It is also very easy to grow, being almost hardy. In the open, it tends to flower in late winter and early spring but it blossoms earlier in the shelter of the conservatory where its long-lasting flowers with their fine perfume can be most fully enjoyed.

category	Fragrant
type	Evergreen shrub
flowers	Clusters of small pale pink flowers, purplish pink in the bud in winter
leaves	Glossy, dark green, edged with a fine line of yellow
height	60–100cm (24–36in)
spread	100cm (36in)
temperature	0°C (32°F)
position	Full sun
planting	In a clay pot that is not too large
compost	Any well-drained slightly alkaline compost. Add extra sharp sand.
care	Stand the pot outside in the summer. Repot in late summer when the year's growth has matured
propagation	Take semi-ripe cuttings preferably with a heel, in summer. Insert in equal parts sand and peat or a proprietary cuttings compost. Cover the pot and place in a cold frame until the following spring. Pot up the rooted cuttings in JI No. 1. Seeds should be sown when ripe (mid-autumn) and kept in a cold frame. Pot on as necessary
species and varieties	*D. bholua* has a more upright habit and is occasionally deciduous

BUDDLEIA ▲
(Buddleia asiatica)

Buddleia asiatica is the most strongly perfumed of the semi-tender buddleias and needs care with pruning. Like all buddleias it is very vigorous and neglect will result in long bare stems with flowers only at the ends.

category	Challenging
type	Evergreen shrub
flowers	Sweetly-scented cream flowers, in typical buddleia-type panicles at the end of arching stems in winter
leaves	Long, narrow grey-green
height	3m (10ft)
spread	3m (10ft)
temperature	0–7°C (32–45°F)
position	Sun or partial shade
planting	30cm (12in) pots
compost	JI No. 2
care	Either train the main stems against a wall and prune to encourage lateral growths that will hang down, or cut back hard in late winter after flowering. It is very susceptible to whitefly
propagation	Take cuttings in late summer from short side shoots and root these in a half peat half sand mixture or a proprietary cuttings compost
species and varieties	*B. tubiflora* has erect spikes of clusters of bright orange tubular flowers and needs a minimum temperature of 7–10°C (45–50°F)

SNOWDROP
(Galanthus nivalis 'Flore Pleno'*)*

Bowls of snowdrops are very worthwhile in a shady conservatory and show to great advantage among the ferns and other foliage plants which also flourish there. *G. nivalis* 'Flore Pleno', the double common snowdrop, has its stamens converted to petals sometimes tipped with green. Many other species and cultivars can be best appreciated in bowls at close quarters.

category	Cool and shady
type	Bulb
flowers	Double white, pendent, 2–2.5cm ($^{3}/_{4}$–1in) long, one on each stem in winter
leaves	Grey-green, narrow
height	10–15cm (4–6in)
spread	5–8cm (2–3in)
temperature	Completely hardy
position	Shade
planting	Pot up as early as possible; 'in the green', as the flowers are dying down in late winter to early spring is best. Put the pots in a shady frame for the summer. Bring them into the conservatory in midwinter
compost	JI No. 2
care	Never allow the pots to dry out completely. Only divide and repot the bulbs when they become overcrowded every three years or so
propagation	The bulbs multiply naturally. They also increase by seed
species and varieties	*G.* 'Atkinsii' can reach 25cm (10in) and has a green spot at the top of each inner petal; *G. nivalis* 'Sandersenii' has flowers with yellow patches; *G.* 'Samuel Arnott' is a vigorous hybrid, with large flowers

CAMELLIA
(Camellia × williamsii 'Debbie'*)*

With glossy, rich green leaves and perfectly formed flowers in pink, white or red, and sometimes deliciously striped, camellias are among the finest plants for the winter conservatory. Even if you can grow them out-of-doors (the plants themselves are hardy although the flowers can be damaged by frost and rain), camellias are worth space in the conservatory. There are dozens of beautiful varieties and species to choose from but 'Debbie' has the virtue of gracefully and tidily dropping its flowers whole before the petals turn brown.

category	Easy
type	Evergreen shrub
flowers	Bright pink, semi-double 6–8cm (2$^{1}/_{2}$–3in) in diameter in winter
leaves	Glossy, leathery
height	2m (6ft)
spread	1.5m (5ft)
temperature	Frost free
position	Semi-shade
planting	20–30cm (8–12in) pots or tubs
compost	Well-drained, ericaceous
care	Water with rainwater and keep the compost moist but not waterlogged, being particularly careful to water thoroughly in mid- to late summer when the shrub is forming its flower buds for the following year. Liquid feed in the growing season (late spring–early summer) with Miracid or other special fertilizer formulated for acid-loving plants. Stand the pot outside in a cool shady place from late spring to late autumn or even later
propagation	Take 10cm (4in) semi-hardwood cuttings, or leaf-bud cuttings in mid- to late summer. Root in equal quantities of peat and sand with a bottom heat of 13–16°C (55–61°F)
species and varieties	*C. japonica* 'Desire' has narrower leaves and exquisitely shaped white petals edged with pink. The flowers of *C. japonica* 'Lavinia Maggi' are flushed with pink and streaked with crimson

practical project

BUILDING A TROUGH
FOR LARGER PLANTS

Incise a building line, marking the front face of the trough

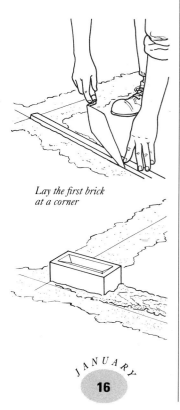

Lay the first brick at a corner

For conservatories without borders but with solid concrete floors, a raised trough provides the root room that many plants thrive in. The trough will need to be about 50–55cm (20–22in) high, and 30–40cm (12–16in) wide. The length depends on the space you have available in the conservatory. It is inadvisable to construct the trough against an internal wall as this might create problems with damp.

YOU WILL NEED

Bricks, Cement, Sand
Spade, Watering can
Chalk, Brick trowel
Bolster, Club hammer for breaking the bricks
Set square or builder's square, Spirit level
Pegs and twine, to mark brick courses
Overflow pipe, for drainage
Waterproofing
A large piece of hardboard or similar to mix the cement on
To fill the trough
hard core, old bricks, stones, for the bottom to ensure good drainage
Fibreglass insulation material
Good compost – JI No. 2 or 3

How many bricks?
It is simple to estimate how many bricks you will need. The working size of a brick (that is the brick plus the mortar joints is 23 x 8 x 11cm (9 x 3 x 4.5in), so a trough 45cm (18in) high will need six courses of bricks. For a wall this high, one thickness of brick laid in stretcher or running bond is quite sufficient.

Making the trough
■ Measure the outline of your trough on the floor and draw it with chalk. Mix the mortar, using a mix of 1 part cement to 3 parts sand. Spread a thin layer of mortar along the outline you have drawn and then using the trowel and a straight edge, incise a building line in the mortar where the front face of the trough will be. Ensure that the right angles are accurate by using a set square or builder's square.

■ Lay another thick layer of mortar at one of the corners, taking care not to obscure the lines in the mortar bed and lay the first corner brick in it. This first brick gives the lines for the rest of the wall.

■ Lay several bricks along both arms of the corner: the 'frogs', or dips, in the brick should be at the top.

■ Then lay several bricks of the second course staggering the bricks so that the joints are not directly above each other. Insert a piece of piping through the wall between the bricks at this level as a 'drain' for excess water. (See finished trough.) Press the bricks down and remove excess mortar as you go.

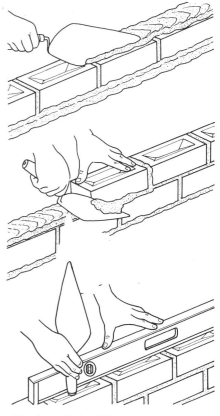

■ Use the spirit level frequently to check for accuracy.

■ Add more layers of bricks to build up the corner as shown. Make frequent checks on the alignment.

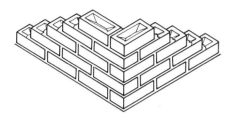

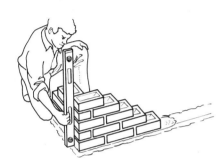

■ Work the opposite corner in the same way. To build the wall that connects the two corners you will need to use pegs and twine to ensure the courses are level.

■ Before mortar hardens, it must be smoothed neatly on the front face (and, if you are making a raised pool by the same procedure, on the inside as well). First smooth the vertical joints, then the horizontal joints. Finally, brush off any excess mortar.

Finishing off

When the walls are complete, finish off the top layer with tiles or lay the final layer of bricks with the frog downwards. After the mortar has dried, it is advisable, (but not essential) to paint the inside of the trough with a waterproofing compound.

Filling the trough

■ Put in a good layer of rubble for drainage.

■ Place a layer of the thinnest fibreglass insulation material between the drainage layer and the compost. This will prevent the finest particles of soil being washed downwards to clog the spaces between the stones.

■ Add the appropriate compost for the plants you plan to grow. Press the compost down, allow it to settle and then add more. Leave sufficient space at the top for watering and mulching.

PLANTS FOR A LARGE TROUGH

Abutilon cvs.
Acacia spp.
Bougainvillea cvs.
Brugmansias
Campsis radicans
Correa backhouseana
Fig 'White Ischia'
Grape vines
Jasmine polyanthum
Lonicera hildebrandtiana
  (Giant honeysuckle)
Mandevilla laxa
Musa spp. (Bananas)
Plumeria rubra (Frangipani)
Prostanthera lasianthos
Strelitzia regina
Streptosolen jamesonii
  (Marmalade Bush)
Thunbergia grandiflora
Tibouchina urvilleana

plants
OF THE
month
2

AUSTRALIAN
PLANTS

CATEGORIES
The plants featured here are in
no particular category. They are
simply an Australian collection
suitable for the conservatory.

ACACIA
(Acacia baileyana)

The Cootamunda wattle is a graceful small
tree with arching branches, cheerful flowers
in winter and beautiful, feathery, glaucous
foliage all year. It even has a light perfume.

type	Small, evergreen tree
flowers	Small puffs of bright yellow stamens in clusters 5–10cm (2–4in) long in winter and early spring
leaves	Blue-grey finely divided
height	2.5m (8ft)
spread	1.8m (6ft)
temperature	0–4°C (32–39°F), will stand a degree or so of frost
position	Sunny
planting	Pots or border
compost	Rich, well-drained. Avoid peat
care	Never let the compost dry out completely. Feed with liquid fertilizer every fortnight from late spring to late summer. To keep plant within bounds, prune new growth immediately after flowering. This acacia must have cold nights and good ventilation in order to flower. Young plants need supporting
propagation	Sow seed in mid-spring at a temperature of 16°C (61°F). When large enough to handle, prick off into 8cm (3in) pots of JI No. 1
species and varieties	A. baileyana 'Purpurea' has foliage tinged with purple. A. dealbata is larger, with silvery leaves and it is even more frost tolerant

CORREA
(Correa backhouseana)

The neat rounded leaves of C. backhouseana are
rough to the touch, like a kitten's tongue, and
they are backed with brown down. Palest yellow bells appear in early spring and continue
for a long season.

type	Medium-sized evergreen shrub
flowers	Creamy yellow, tubular bells, 2.5cm (1in) long in early spring
leaves	Oval, dark green with light brown down beneath
height	2m (6ft)
spread	2m (6ft)
temperature	3–4°C (37–39°F)
position	Full sun or some shade
planting	Pots or border
compost	Well-drained neutral to acid
care	Do not overwater plants that are in

pots and avoid using hard water.
Cut back plants by two-thirds after
they have flowered if they get too
leggy

propagation	Sow seed in spring or take semi-ripe cuttings in late summer. They are not difficult to strike
species and varieties	C. 'Mannii' is showier, with light red bell flowers from winter to spring. C. pulchella has delicate pink bells

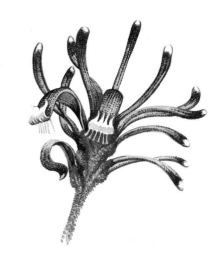

KANGAROO PAW
(Anigozanthos manglesii)

Green tubular flowers on a stalk covered in
velvety red down make Mangles' kangaroo
paw a striking specimen for the conservatory.

type	Evergreen perennial
flowers	7cm (3in) long, furry, bright green and red tubes, that split into claw-like segments at the end, in early summer
leaves	Fans of iris-like leaves
height	60–100cm (24–36in)
spread	45cm (18in)
temperature	4°C (39°F)
position	Sunny but shade flowers from hottest sun
planting	23cm (9in) pot
compost	Well-drained, peaty acid compost with some loam
care	Good ventilation. Water well with soft water in spring and summer but only moderately during winter. Liquid feed from midsummer onwards
propagation	Easy by seed, which is

recommended for this species. Care needed with fleshy roots if dividing in spring. Slow to re-establish afterwards

species and varieties	*A. flavidus* has yellow-green flowers with reddish anthers

BORONIA
(Boronia megastigma)

This bushy, wiry-stemmed evergreen shrub is grown for its unusually-coloured, fragrant flowers in late winter.

type	Evergreen shrub
flowers	Small, very fragrant purple-brown and gold flowers in the leaf axils in late winter
leaves	Narrow, tiny, aromatic
height	75cm (30in)
spread	75cm (30in)
temperature	4°C (39°F)
position	Sun or semi-shade. Dislikes too much heat
planting	Needs a cool root run and dislikes disturbance to its shallow roots
compost	Ericaceous, peat-based
care	Mulch pots well. Prune back after flowering – but not into old wood – to keep compact. Water frequently, and in hot weather spray leaves as well. Never allow the plants to dry out. Use soft water and a liquid fertilizer formulated for acid-loving plants. Avoid high nitrogen fertilizers
propagation	Take semi-ripe cuttings from lateral shoots in summer. Root in a well-firmed, half peat and half sand

mixture. A very gentle bottom heat will help but the top must be kept cool, at about 10°C (50°F)

species and varieties	*B. megastigma* 'Heaven Scent' is exceptionally fragrant. *B. heterophylla* has profuse delicate pink flowers later in the year

MINT BUSH
(Prostanthera rotundifolia)

The Australian mint bush flowers in summer unlike many Australian native plants. Completely smothered in the dainty mauve flowers in summer, the aromatic leaves are attractive all year.

type	Evergreen shrub
flowers	Profuse, small bell-shaped flowers of lavender- to purple-blue in late spring
leaves	Small, rounded and mint-scented
height	1.8m (6ft)
spread	1–1.2m (3–4ft)
temperature	2–7°C (36–45°F)
position	Semi-shade
planting	Large pot 24–30cm (9–12in), or border
compost	Moist but well-drained, fertile
care	Avoid overwatering in winter. Prune lightly after flowering
propagation	Sow seed in spring or take semi-ripe cuttings in late summer
species and varieties	*P. cuneata* is smaller and has white-mauve flowers. *P. lasianthos* has large white flowers

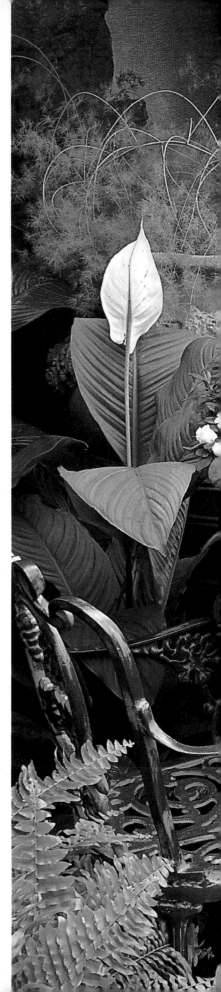

FEBRUARY

Sweetly scented jasmine, J. polyanthum, *with its white flowers, pink in bud, dripping from the roof of the conservatory, is the star of this month. It is one of the many useful plants that can be bought inexpensively as a flowering pot plant (often in early winter), and then planted out into the conservatory border to flower again, but rather later, the following year.* Camellia × williamsii *'Debbie' is in flower but by now may be dropping its blooms so that they lie on the floor like lipstick-pink tutus. These two have been joined by chionodoxa, crocus,* Iris reticulata, I. danfordiae *and other small bulbs that can often flower unseen in the garden if the weather is too cold to spend much time there. Pots and containers of recently germinated fritillaries, dierama and tulbaghia are showing delicate spears which, if they have been grown from seed, can seem as exciting as plants in full bloom. In the gradually increasing warmth, tiny snails that have come in attached to the bottom of a plant pot will glide about looking for tender things to eat. Watch out for them. Whitefly may be on the increase, so flowers will be joined by strategically placed yellow sticky cards. Quick action now keeps the problem to manageable proportions. This is the time of year when the temptation to use the conservatory as a greenhouse begins. The sand bench warmed with heating cables, which has been used to keep tender plants alive during the coldest nights, can also be used for germinating seeds. Seeds sown in small covered pots can be easily insinuated among the mature plants without spoiling any decorative effect. A simple cold frame next to the conservatory is worth considering at this stage if the conservatory is not to lose its purpose as a place for people to relax in as well as for the display of plants.*

tasks

FOR THE

month

NOTE
Abutilon prunings can be used
for cuttings if you choose young,
sturdy shoots and root them
round the edge of a 7cm (3in) pot
using a proprietary compost
especially for cutting or JI No. 1.
When the cutting has rooted, pot
on into JI No. 2

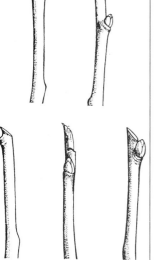

CORRECT AND INCORRECT
PRUNING CUTS
(clockwise from top left) Correct –
an upward cut made just above a
bud; incorrect – sloping towards
the bud and too far above the bud;
incorrect – cut right on the bud;
incorrect – a rough cut; incorrect –
cut sloping towards the bud

CHECKLIST

☐ Prune greenhouse climbers and wall plants
☐ Sow seeds
☐ Plant summer-flowering tubers
☐ Top dress shrubs
☐ Pot on autumn-sown annuals

PRUNING GREENHOUSE CLIMBERS AND WALL PLANTS

Greenhouse climbers can be pruned at any convenient time after flowering between late autumn and early spring (see Tasks for the Month p.123 for illustrations). Winter-flowering climbers will need to be pruned during spring. As with all pruning, cut off any dead or diseased branches. Weak branches or those which cross will also need to be cut out.

Abutilons should have all laterals pruned back to 7.5–10cm (3–4in). Bougainvilleas can be pruned now, but see under Plants of the Month pp.106–107 for special treatment to produce four separate flowering periods. Let the plant develop several main stems and stop these when they are the height required. This encourages the production of flowering side shoots. Prune these side branches back to within two buds of the main stems in late winter to keep the plant compact.

Buddleias need cutting hard back after flowering. Cissus can be trimmed now to keep them tidy but can also be cut hard back if they have become bare at the base. *Maurandya barclayana* and *Eccremocarpus scaber*, the Chilean glory vine, can also be pruned almost to the base (or they can be replaced by new plants from spring-sown seed). Passion flowers need regular pruning at this time to keep them within bounds. You may need to cut some stems right out at ground level; lateral shoots can be cut back to 15cm (6in) at the same time. *Plumbago auriculata* can be treated in the same way. All stems of *Tweedia caerulea* should be reduced by two thirds to encourage new flowering shoots.

Do not prune pandoreas or daphnes unless absolutely necessary. Many other Australian plants such as grevilleas, callistemons and acacias do not require regular pruning.

NOTE

- *Make sure your secateurs are sharp* ■

- *Parrot-bill secateurs are ideal for detailed work in the conservatory* ■

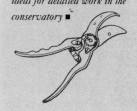

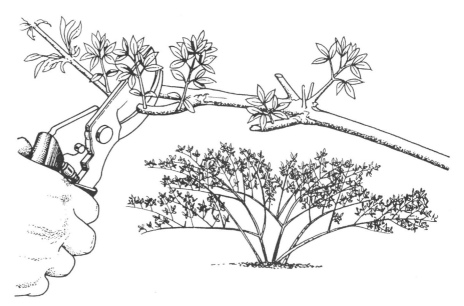

SOWING SEEDS

While you hardly want to turn your conservatory into a greenhouse, it is quite possible to use a propagator to produce eye-catching displays of annual and perennial plants without destroying the 'living-room-with-plants' atmosphere of the conservatory.

By sowing small amounts of seed in 7cm (3in) square pots it is possible to germinate fifteen different varieties in the space of one seed tray. There will still be at least two dozen seedlings in each pot, which will provide sufficient plants to cover average needs plus accidents and still leave some to give away (see margin for seed suggestions).

■ Fill each pot two-thirds full with any good seed compost. Firm it down slightly and then fill the remainder of the pot to within 1cm (¹/₂in) of the top with horticultural vermiculite.

■ Sow the seed finely on top. Unless the seed needs light and air to germinate, as begonia seed does, sprinkle a further fine layer of vermiculite over it.

■ Water the seed in using a very fine rose. Label the pots clearly and put them in a propagator or cover them with a plastic bag, or use the cut-off end of a square plastic bottle and put them on the heated bench or in the airing cupboard.

■ Vermiculite absorbs liquid readily, making watering very simple; it is also very easy to prick out the seedlings.

■ When the seedlings have begun to grow well and are filling the pot it is time to prick them out – see page 34.

■ Buying plug plants, baby plants or pots of germinated

seedlings is a good alternative. Growing them on yourself is much cheaper than buying trays of bedding plants. However, you may not be able to get the varieties you want.

SUMMER-FLOWERING TUBERS

Start begonia tubers into growth by placing them with the concave side upwards, 2.5cm (1in) deep in a tray of damp sandy compost (half

sand and half peat or peat substitute) kept at a minimum temperature of 13–16°C (55–61°F).

Although gloxinias (*Sinningia speciosa* and its hybrids) are frequently raised from seed or propagated from leaf cuttings, they can be grown from stored tubers which are overwintered like dahlia tubers. They need a less sandy compost than begonias and should be placed in small pots in a temperature of 18°C (64°F). They will need potting on when the pot is almost filled with roots.

The tiny tubercles of *Achimenes* can be started into growth in batches, beginning now and continuing until mid-spring. Put them in a light sandy compost at a temperature of 15–18°C (59–64°F) until the shoots are 5cm (2in) high. Then pot up 10 or 12 plants to a 20cm (8in) pot.

TOP DRESS SHRUBS IN POTS

If the roots of a mature plant entirely fill its container covering the soil ball, it may need repotting.

If it does not, then it should be top dressed in spring as growth is starting. Scrape away any mulch and the top layer (2.5cm/1–2in) of compost. Replace with fresh compost and slow release fertilizer or a little blood, fish and bone.

POT ON AUTUMN-SOWN ANNUALS

Autumn-sown hardy annuals which have been standing outside will need potting on this month. A check to their growth will result in premature flowering. The aim is to get the plant as large as possible before it flowers. Re-pot into one size larger pots using JI No. 2 compost. Pinch out growing points.

plants
OF THE
month
1

BERGENIA
(Bergenia 'Silberlicht'*)*

Bergenias are usually planted out-of-doors in some shady neglected spot. If cherished in an unheated conservatory, however, *Bergenia* 'Silberlicht' will surprise you with its magnificent leaves, which make a wonderful foil to the narrow foliage of early flowering bulbs and bold spikes of almost white flowers.

category	Easy
type	Evergreen perennial
flowers	Clusters of white bell-shaped flowers with pale pink calyces on erect stems in late winter/early spring
leaves	Thick, heart-shaped, leathery, may turn red-bronze
height	30cm (12in)
spread	50cm (20in)
temperature	0°C (32°F)
position	Near the window. They are quite hardy and full sun makes the leaves colour to red-bronze
planting	15cm (6in) pot
compost	JI No. 2
care	Repot when necessary. Stand outside in shady spot during the summer
propagation	Divide and replant in spring or early autumn
species and varieties	*B. ciliata* has rounded hairy leaves and white flowers that age to pink. *B.* 'Wintermärchen' has bright pink flowers and smaller, red-tinged leaves. Look out for *B. emeiensis*, recently introduced, which has loose sprays of bell-shaped snow-white flowers with a green eye

CROTON
(Codiaeum variegatum var. *pictum)*

Crotons are frequently sold as foliage house-plants. They have bright variegated, lobed leaves in a variety of colours and patterns.

category	Challenging
type	Evergreen shrub
flowers	None
leaves	Glossy, leathery, varying in size, shape and colour with age and light. They can be variegated with red, pink, yellow and orange
height	1.5m (5ft)
spread	1m (3ft)
temperature	13–16°C (55–61°F) minimum
position	Shade from hot sun. Keep out of draughts

planting	13–18cm (5–7in) pots in spring
compost	JI No. 2
care	It is preferable to keep crotons at a steady low temperature rather than to subject them to fluctuating temperatures if the optimum heat cannot be retained. They need a humid atmosphere and are susceptible to draughts. Keep compact if necessary by pruning hard in spring
propagation	Take 8cm (3in) tip cuttings between spring and early summer. Dip them in powdered charcoal to prevent milky sap 'bleeding'. Root in propagator at 24°C (75°F)
species and varieties	Although many good named varieties exist, most crotons on sale are varieties of *Codiaeum variegatum* var. *pictum*. Select the variegation you like best

DAFFODIL
(Narcissus 'Silver Chimes'*)*

After snowdrops, early daffodils brighten a shady conservatory. *N.* 'Silver Chimes' is a sturdy tazetta or bunch-flowered hybrid narcissus, one of a group that flourishes in warmth and is known for its fragrance.

category	Cool and shady
type	Bulb
flowers	Milky-white petals, creamy-yellow cup; up to ten small flowers on a stem
leaves	Dark green
height	32cm (13in)

temperature	10–18°C (50–64°F) for flowering
position	Any
planting	Plant bulbs in early autumn, five bulbs to a 12cm (5in) pot. Put them in a dark cool place for two months, then bring into unheated conservatory. Extra warmth after three weeks will encourage them to bloom if the temperature in the conservatory is not reaching the required level
compost	JI No. 2 with a drainage layer in the base of the pot
care	Remove flower stems after flowering but continue to water. Feed with a high potash feed until leaves die down, then leave the bulbs undisturbed in a dry cool place until it is time to repot them in the following autumn
propagation	Remove offsets from the bulbs and plant separately. They should reach flowering size in one or two years
species and varieties	*N.* 'Minnow' is 18cm (7in) high; *N. canaliculatus* has white, reflexed petals and a dark yellow cup; *N. romieuxii* is 10cm (4in) high with large, delicate cups; *N. asturiensis* has tiny yellow trumpets 2.5cm (1in) long; *N. rupicola* is another dwarf species with a flat yellow cup; *N. bulbocodium* var. *conspicuus*, one of the hoop-petticoat daffodils, is another miniature at 8–15cm (3–6in) tall; *N. triandrus* has drooping milky-white flowers with a long cup. These small species narcissi have to be bought from specialist bulb firms but are worth seeking out

JASMINE
(Jasminum polyanthum)

When the Chinese jasmine with its hundreds of heavily perfumed flowers is in bloom in the depths of winter, it makes even the worst weather bearable. It is widely available as a pot plant, often trained round a circular frame. This is a good way to acquire one although larger plants can be bought from nurseries. In an unheated conservatory, the jasmine will not flower as early as it does when forced for the pot plant market and it may take a year to settle down.

category	Fragrant
type	Evergreen climber
flowers	Small white flowers, often pink on the outside, in large clusters

leaves	Dark green leaves made up of five or seven leaflets
height	3m (10ft) or more
spread	1–1.5m (3–5ft)
temperature	3–7°C (37–45°F)
position	Cool, but in good light
planting	Best in the border but also 25–30cm (10–12in) pots
compost	JI No. 2
care	Train *J. polyanthum* up wires, pillars or strings to the conservatory roof. It needs a period of cold for setting buds. Do not allow the plant to get dry at the roots, particularly during the bud stage. Prune hard back after flowering: you will need to take woody stems down from whatever they have been attached to and prune them hard back to 5–8cm (2–3in) – prunings can be used as cuttings. Younger branches can be shortened to where there are healthy side-shoots. Tie the stems back to the frame or wires. Liquid feed from spring until autumn only and do not over-fertilize
propagation	Take heel cuttings of semi-ripe wood during late summer. Insert into cutting compost or equal parts of peat and sand, and root with a bottom heat of 16°C (61°F)
species and varieties	*J. officinale* is very vigorous and hardy and flowers in summer; *J. primulinum* has yellow flowers in spring

practical project 1

SIMPLE TRELLIS
SUPPORT

PLANTS FOR GROWING UP A SMALL TRELLIS

Clianthus puniceus (Parrot's bill)
Gloriosa superba
Hardenbergia violacea
Ipomoea indica (Perennial morning glory)
Jasminum sambac (Arabian jasmine)
Lophospermum erubescens
L. scandens
Maurandya barclayana
Mutisia decurrens
M. ilicifolia
Senecio macroglossus
'Variegatus' (Variegated Cape ivy)
Sollya heterophylla (Bluebell creeper)
Tweedia caerulea

NOTE
Imperial measurements given are not exact conversions but are the equivalents as used by most hardware stores selling wood.

Growing climbers is the quickest way of creating a lavish, well-planted look in a conservatory. There are many ways of supporting them, including ready-made simple plastic netting or trellis, wires fixed to the wall with vine eyes, and elaborate patterns of trellis work. Climbers can also be free-standing, supported on a moss pole, bamboo canes or classic obelisk. Providing supports can be an opportunity to add striking effects to your indoor garden.

If you plan to paint your fan trellis, and this looks very effective, buy smooth-planed battens. You will find it much much easier to paint them before assembling the structure. The lighter cross pieces do not need to be exactly the size suggested but adjustments will have to be made if the width differs significantly.

YOU WILL NEED

- *Three lengths of wood 44mm (1³/₄in) square for the frame. Divide these into:*
One main upright 2m (6ft) long with an extra 38cm (15in), for sinking into the border or into concrete (A). (If this is going to be fixed directly on to a wall, it can be shorter.)
Two cross pieces. One 40cm (16in approx) and one 80cm (32in approx) (B).
- *Battens 22 x 19mm (⁷/₈ x ³/₄in) for the cross pieces. Cut the first cross piece 44cm (17³/₄in) wide then make each of the following nine pieces 3.5cm (1³/₄in) longer than the previous one. Altogether you will need three lengths of batten: two 2m (80in) and one 3m (10ft) will be sufficient if you cut the largest cross piece and the two smallest from one 2m (80in) piece, the second largest and the next two smallest from the second 2m (80in) piece and the remaining four cross pieces from the 3m (10ft) length of batten.*
- *Five lengths of 22 x 19mm (⁷/₈ x ³/₄in) timber 2m (80in) long for the final verticals (C).*

Other items
Rustproof nails, Staples, Screws, Dowelling
Wood glue, Tenon saw, Hammer
Wood preservative **OR**
Undercoat **AND** *Paint for top coat*
Masonry bolts
Electric drill with a bit larger than the diameter of the bolts
Spirit level, Tape measure

- First, fix the two sturdy cross pieces (B) to the upright (A), as shown. Glue these joints and screw from the back.

- Then fix the batten cross pieces, with the narrowest at the bottom and the widest at the top. The gap between the pieces should be 152mm (6in). Don't forget that the battens are 19mm (³/₄in) wide. Put the tape measure on the top of the bottom batten, measure 152mm (6in) and draw a line. That is where the bottom edge of the next cross piece goes. Glue the piece on lightly, making sure it is properly centred and level. Then screw firmly into the centre upright. Continue until the cross pieces are complete.

- Finally, fix the remaining uprights (C) in position, starting with the centrepiece.

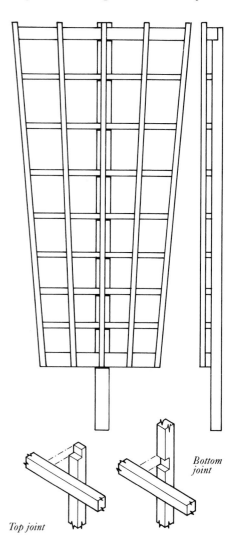

Bottom joint

Top joint

Screw this firmly to the top and bottom and use wood glue to attach it to the battens in between. Then fix the outside battens. Screw on firmly to the sturdy cross pieces at the top and bottom. The remaining battens can be fixed with strong wood glue and/or small nails or staples. When placing the final two battens take care that they are symmetrical.

■ When the trellis is completed it should be fixed to the wall with two masonry bolts. Drill holes into the upright, one-third from the top and one-third from the bottom. Hold it up against the wall and mark where the holes come. Then drill holes into the wall larger than the diameter of the screw. Fill the holes with pieces of dowelling or roughly shaped wood and then hold the frame in place and screw the masonry bolts in. Because the trellis is inside, it will not need to be as firmly fixed as if it were outside and subject to strong winds.

Now you have made this simple trellis support, why not try your hand at an obelisk or archway.

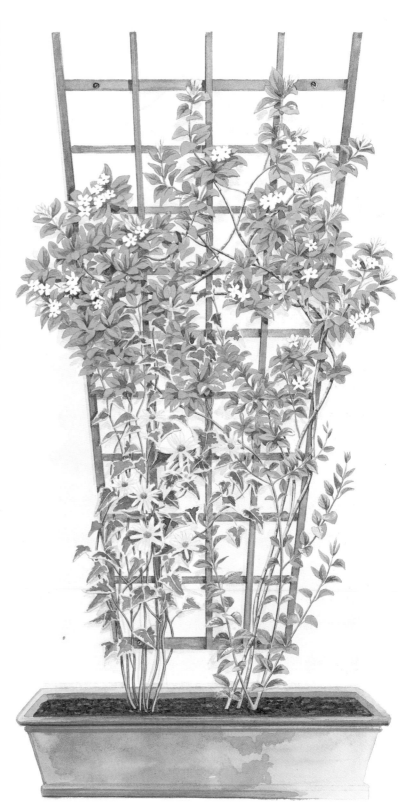

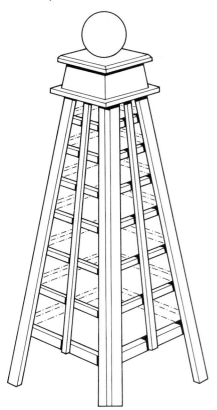

You can make a simple obelisk by joining four pieces of trellis as shown here

plants
OF THE
month
2

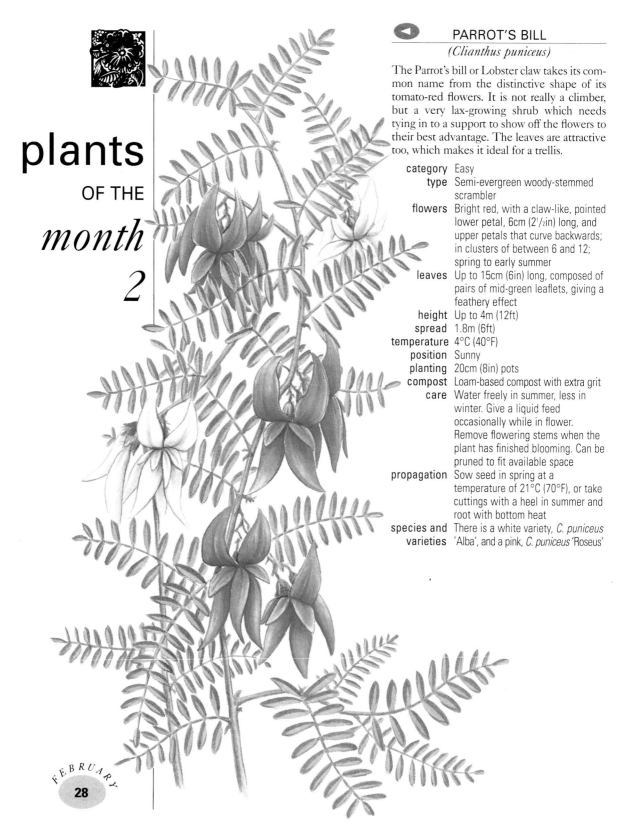

PARROT'S BILL
(Clianthus puniceus)

The Parrot's bill or Lobster claw takes its common name from the distinctive shape of its tomato-red flowers. It is not really a climber, but a very lax-growing shrub which needs tying in to a support to show off the flowers to their best advantage. The leaves are attractive too, which makes it ideal for a trellis.

category	Easy
type	Semi-evergreen woody-stemmed scrambler
flowers	Bright red, with a claw-like, pointed lower petal, 6cm (2½in) long, and upper petals that curve backwards; in clusters of between 6 and 12; spring to early summer
leaves	Up to 15cm (6in) long, composed of pairs of mid-green leaflets, giving a feathery effect
height	Up to 4m (12ft)
spread	1.8m (6ft)
temperature	4°C (40°F)
position	Sunny
planting	20cm (8in) pots
compost	Loam-based compost with extra grit
care	Water freely in summer, less in winter. Give a liquid feed occasionally while in flower. Remove flowering stems when the plant has finished blooming. Can be pruned to fit available space
propagation	Sow seed in spring at a temperature of 21°C (70°F), or take cuttings with a heel in summer and root with bottom heat
species and varieties	There is a white variety, *C. puniceus* 'Alba', and a pink, *C. puniceus* 'Roseus'

DEVIL'S IVY ▼
(Epipremnum aureum)

A woody-stemmed root climber grown for its large, handsome, variegated leaves. It produces aerial roots, which makes it particularly suitable for growing up a moss pole, but it can also be grown simply in a pot, with a support. In its natural habitat, in the Solomon Islands, it can reach 12m (40ft) with leaves up to 45cm (18in) long.

category	Cool and shady
type	Evergreen climber
flowers	Green spathes when mature
leaves	Heart-shaped glossy leaves splashed with yellow
height	1.8–3m (6–10ft)
spread	1.8–3m (6–10ft)
temperature	15°C (59°F)
position	Shade
planting	On a moss pole (see p.28) or in a 20–25cm (8–10in) pot, according to the size you want the plant to grow
compost	JI No. 2 with added peat and grit
care	Devil's ivy is easy to cultivate and will stand a certain amount of dryness and draught. It will not flourish if over-watered or if the air is too dry. Water regularly, less in cold weather. Remove shoot tips to encourage branching. Shoots need tying in
propagation	The shoot tips root easily, as do sections of stem containing two nodes
species and varieties	*E. aureum* 'Marble Queen' has leaves that are heavily marbled almost white. *Scindapsus pictus*, the Silver vine, has similar shaped leaves, spotted and clouded with a lighter green

VINE LILAC ▶
(Hardenbergia violacea)

An Australian climber, also known as Australian sarsparilla, vine lilac is grown for its curtains of leaves and masses of dark lilac-coloured flowers in late winter and early spring. It is perfect for a large trellis in a trough or raised bed.

category	Challenging
type	Evergreen, twining climber
flowers	Deep lilac-mauve pea-flowers in racemes; late winter and early spring
leaves	Narrow oval, between 2.5 and 12cm (1 and 5in) long
height	1.8–3m (6–10ft)
spread	1m (3ft)
temperature	7°C (45°F)
position	Sun
planting	Best in a trough or raised bed as it dislikes drying out
compost	JI No. 2 with added grit
care	Repot or top dress every year in summer. Keep well watered during flowering time and prune afterwards
propagation	Seed, soaked before sowing, in spring or stem cuttings in late summer
species and varieties	*H. violacea* 'White Crystal' and *H. violacea* 'Rosea' are white and pink respectively. 'Happy Wanderer' is a good form while *H. comptoniana* is similar to *H. violacea* but has deep purple-blue flowers

practical
project
2

MAKING
A MOSS POLE

Plants with aerial roots look dramatic and flourish particularly well with the extra moisture provided by a sturdy support packed with damp moss.

YOU WILL NEED

Sphagnum moss
A length of chicken wire 45cm (18in) wide by
1–1.5m (3–5ft) long
Broom handle
Long stick, Small staples
Hammer, Pliers
Large sturdy plant pot
Stones, Compost

■ The broom handle provides support for the chicken wire. Fix the wire to the handle in one or two places with small staples and roll it round to make a cylinder about 8cm (3in) in diameter, securing the end of the chicken wire to the handle.

■ Fill the cylinder with the moss. Use a long stick to tamp the moss down or fill the cylinder through the holes in the netting.

■ Insert the moss pole deeply into the pot and wedge with stones, leaving room for the rootball of your selected plant.

■ Put the plant in and then fill the pot with good compost.

■ To work properly the moss must be kept damp. A moss pole makes a good support for plants with aerial roots, like monsteras, scindapsus *(Epipremnum)* and philodendrons.

AFTERCARE

A moss pole can dry out quickly so needs frequent misting and watering if it is to work well: the colour of the moss will tell you when watering is required – if it is dark green, it is damp enough, but if the moss begins to turn pale and yellowish, mist and water the moss pole without delay. If the plants growing up the pole need feeding, use a weak foliar feed.

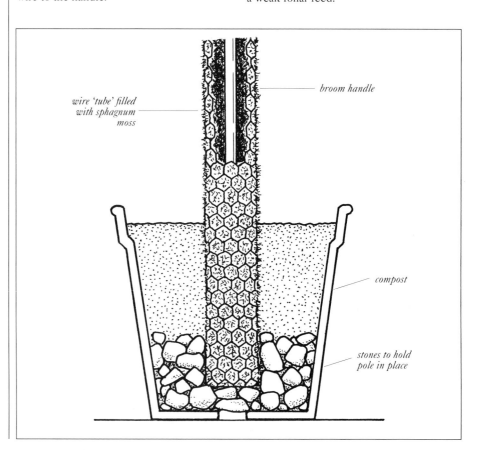

wire 'tube' filled with sphagnum moss

broom handle

compost

stones to hold pole in place

**PLANTS FOR GROWING
ON MOSS POLES**

Cheese plant *(Monstera deliciosa)*
Devil's ivy *(Scindapsus* or
   Epipremnum)
Hare's foot fern *(Davallia
   canariensis)* is an epiphytic fern
Ivies *(Hedera helix* spp.*)*
Philodendron erubescens
P. erubescens 'Imperial Red'
Silver vine *(Scindapsus pictus)*

MARCH

The first month of spring is the busiest time of the year for gardeners, indoors and out. The difference is that out-of-doors, nature does some of the work, blowing away dead leaves and watering the plants. In the conservatory you have to do this. This is a wonderful excuse for spending a lot of time there, out of the rain and cold but among plants. Last month's star plant, Jasminum polyanthum *will still be in flower while* Pittosporum tobira, *the deliciously scented mock orange is coming into bloom. Both of these make the conservatory an irresistible place to be.*

The days are longer but the weather is still highly unpredictable. Even on grey days, however, the light is much brighter in the conservatory and the plants are responding. The extra light intensity will do you as much good as it does the plants.

When you go to your nearest garden centre, garden shop, supermarket or DIY store, look out for displays of 'dot' plants. For less than £1 you can buy tiny tropical foliage plants such as Chamaedorea, Strobilanthes, Gynura, Dracaena, Codiaeum *(crotons)* and Asparagus plumosus *(asparagus fern) to try out in the conservatory. Like all babies they need tender loving care to start with but it is a very inexpensive way of experimenting with what will or will not 'do' in your particular conservatory. If they flourish, they will add vivid purples, brilliant reds and glowing yellow foliage, as well as contrasts of shape and texture to your plant display.*

This is the month when it seems as if spring will never come. In the conservatory, however, whatever the weather is like outside, it can be full of flowering spring bulbs. If your conservatory isn't, make a note in your diary to remedy this and buy bulbs in late summer. Tiny jonquil narcissi have a delightful scent. Miniature irises, species crocus and tulips all come in a wide range of colours. Early flowering Tulipa humilis 'Violacea' *goes particularly well with the blue-pinks of camellias, cyclamen and azaleas.*

tasks
FOR THE
month

SEEDS FOR SOWING

Browallia various
Convolvulus tricolor
Gerbera jamesonii
Limonium various
Nemesia various
Phlox drummondii
Schizanthus – the poor man's orchid or butterfly flower will make smaller, later flowering plants if sown now, than they do with an autumn sowing

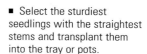

CHECKLIST

- ☐ Prick out and pot on
- ☐ Water
- ☐ Feed

PRICKING OUT

If you are pricking out a pot of seedlings, water them and the fresh compost beforehand with a solution of Cheshunt compound. This prevents 'damping-off', a fungal disease which causes seedlings to topple over and die. You can avoid damaging the stems when pricking out seedlings or potting up very young plants, by never handling the stems of the plants. Hold the seed leaves instead.

- To prick out seedlings, fill a plant tray or small 6cm (2¹/₂in) pots with a soil-based potting compost.

- Firm the compost to remove any air pockets and make small holes in the centre with a dibber.

- Loosen the seedlings in their tray or pot by knocking the container against a hard surface.

- Using an old teaspoon or knife, separate the seedlings out, keeping as much compost as possible around their roots

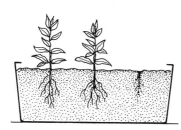

- Select the sturdiest seedlings with the straightest stems and transplant them into the tray or pots.

- Firm the compost round them with your fingertips and water each one in gently.

- Keep the seedlings covered with a transparent lid or cloche for a few days while they recover.

POTTING ON

After pricking out comes potting on. Traditionally it was believed that plants should be potted on into a pot only one size larger. However, recent trials with fuchsias, pansies and marigolds carried out by *Gardening Which?* seem to indicate that they do better if planted straight from a small 6cm (2¹/₂in) pot into a 15cm (6in) pot, though the plants took a little longer to get into their stride. The best display for fuchsias was achieved with three plants potted up directly into a 15cm (6in) pot. The fuchsias were not fed until the roots had completely filled the pot.

- To pot on a plant, water it well one hour beforehand.

- Make sure the fresh compost is moist.

- Fill the larger containers very lightly with new compost and use the old pot to make an indentation in it.

- Then spread your hand over the plant pot, holding the plant stem between two fingers, and tip the pot upside down.

- Tap the bottom of the pot sharply and the plant should come out. If it does not, tap the rim of the pot on a hard surface. If that fails, slide a knife round the inside of the pot.

- Once free of the old pot place the plant in the indentation in the new pot.

- Do not fill the pot too full (it makes it difficult to water) and ensure that the plant is at the same depth in the compost as it was in the previous pot.

Some shrubs in containers where the mouth of the pot is smaller than the body can be removed for replanting by sliding a pruning saw down

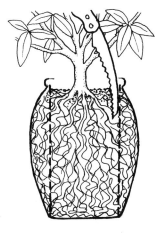

inside the pot and sawing round the roots. Check first that the shrub to be extracted in this drastic way does not object to root disturbance! The alternative is to smash the pot.

Some plants, on the other hand, like being pot-bound, for example *Cyrtanthus elata*, (the Scarborough lily), *Clivia miniata*, hippeastrums and members of the pea family, such as cassia and polygala. These will need to be top dressed instead. (See p.23.)

WATERING

Watering can be increased this month for plants that are actively growing. To check if a plant needs watering press your thumb well into the compost. It is easy to be misled if the surface appears dry, particularly with coconut fibre composts. Some plants, like cyclamen, should be watered from below to avoid splashing the corms. Do this by standing the pots in water until the compost is damp and dark in colour.

To water a wilting plant in a dried-out peat compost, immerse the container completely in a bucket of water. Leave it in the water until the air bubbles stop rising. This will revive many plants. Hydrangeas, polygala and leptospermums in pots must be kept moist as they cannot survive dryness at the roots.

If a plant is wilting and the soil is very moist, then it has probably been *over*watered. Remove the plant and compost from the container for twenty-four hours if you can, to let the compost dry out and air reach the roots.

Points to remember

■ Water well but not too often. In winter, when plants are dormant, twice a month may be enough.

■ More plants in pots die from overwatering than from underwatering.

■ Plant roots need air as well as water.

FEEDING

A weak liquid feed can be given to growing plants this month. Use half-strength feed once a fortnight to start with. *Never* use a more concentrated solution than the manufacturer recommends as this can damage the plant's roots. Plants that have been repotted or top dressed will not need additional liquid fertilizer for six to eight weeks. Do not feed very dry plants as it may damage their roots. Also, delay feeding hard pruned plants until new growth appears.

Fertilizers

■ *Liquid feeds* can be either a powder which is dissolved in water or a concentrated liquid which has to be diluted. Many fertilizers that are applied as a liquid can also be used as foliar feeds. Epiphytes have to be fed through their leaves by misting them with water containing a very dilute liquid fertilizer. Other plants too benefit from an occasional quick-acting foliar tonic. Always follow the manufacturer's instructions when using any fertilizer.

■ *Slow release fertilizers* are the granules, spikes or tablets which are put into the soil and dissolve very slowly when the temperature and moisture are correct. Granules have to be mixed in when the plant is potted up. Spikes or tablets can be pushed into the soil at any time.

■ *Organic fertilizers* such as bone meal, blood fish and bone and calcified seaweed can be used in the potting mixture or as top dressing. Dried blood and pelleted chicken manure have a strong smell and are not ideal for the enclosed space of a conservatory.

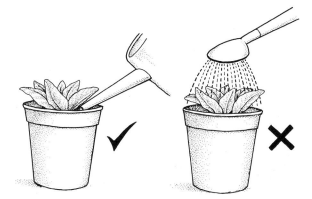

ROUTINE TASKS

Ventilate regularly in the middle of the day unless temperature is below 5°C (41°F)

Shade large-leaved plants and tiny seedlings from hot midday sun

Pot on autumn-sown annuals into 13cm (5in) pots

Prick out seeds sown last month as soon as they are large enough to handle

Divide Canna lilies

Cut back bushy, mature pelargoniums

Buy fresh hormone rooting powder

Fuchsias and hydrangeas started into growth last month may have produced shoots that could be used for cuttings

Start tubers of begonia and sinningias (gloxinias) into growth, if not done last month

Hand-pollinate fruit (see p.103)

DISBUD FRUIT
Mature peaches and nectarines that have filled their available space will need disbudding. Small side shoots that form on the fruiting laterals are pinched off, leaving only one side shoot at the base of the lateral and one at the end

TRAIN GRAPES
If you are seriously growing grape vines for fruit and not as ornamental plants, the young laterals of each vine must be pulled down gradually so that they can be trained along the horizontal wires

plants
OF THE
month
1

FAN PALM
(Chamaerops humilis)

Palm trees produce an instant tropical effect in the conservatory and the European fan palm is one of the easiest to grow. Out-of-doors it can reach 6m (20ft) but in a pot may only grow to a quarter of that. The striking fan-shaped leaves emerge straight from the soil. As new leaves grow, the older ones die and fall off, eventually forming a stiff fibre-covered trunk. To the novice, palms can look very similar. Read the label carefully to ensure that the right one is selected for aspect and for the space available.

category	Easy
type	Evergreen palm
flowers	Tiny yellow flowers in summer
leaves	Fan-shaped leaves up to 60cm (24in) across
height	1.5m (5ft)
spread	1.5m (5ft)
temperature	4°C (39°F)
position	Full sun

planting	18cm (7in) pot. A self-watering pot is ideal
compost	JI No. 2 with extra sand and leafmould if available
care	In summer the palm must be kept moist at all times. Small palms will need watering at least three times a week; large plants daily. Spray with soft water every week and feed weekly in summer with house-plant food. Repot in spring each year until the plant is almost full size, then pot into a 50cm (20in) container. After that an annual top dressing will be necessary. Clean older leaves with a damp sponge occasionally but never use leaf-shine as it will damage the leaves
propagation	Detach and pot up suckers in late spring. For seed propagation see p.76
species and varieties	Another plant with a similar appearance is the Chinese fan palm or *Livistona chinensis*. This too is almost hardy but must have shade in summer and a richer soil. *Rhapis excelsa*, the lady palm, also needs some shade in summer. It has much smaller leaves, needs perfect drainage and slightly higher temperatures. *Howea forsteriana*, known as the paradise palm, is shade tolerant and can grow to more than 3m (10ft) even in a pot. It should have a minimum winter temperature of 10°C (50°F). The pygmy date palm, *Phoenix roebelinii*, has soft, elegant fronds and usually grows to only 60cm (2ft) high

BIRD OF PARADISE FLOWER
(Strelitzia reginae)

This is one of the most dramatic perennials, with its large, oval leaves on long stalks, not unlike those of a banana (to which it is related). The unmistakable flowers look as if an exotic bird with gaudy plumage has just landed on top of the tall stems. It may take up to six years to flower from seed.

category	Challenging
type	Evergreen perennial
flowers	Orange and blue flowers emerge like a tuft of feathers from a long, beak-like bract
leaves	Fans of large, oval, blue-green leaves on long stalks
height	1m (3ft) or more
spread	75cm (30in)
temperature	5–10°C (40–50°F)

position	Full sun most of year but light shading to prevent scorching of leaves in summer
planting	Border or 20–30cm (8–12in) pots
compost	JI No. 3
care	Water freely in spring and summer but decrease from early autumn. Liquid feed at fortnightly intervals from late spring to early autumn. Pot on or repot every second year in early spring, or after flowering
propagation	Divide suckers in spring or propagate by seed. Seed is cheap but it takes four to six years for the plants to flower
species and varieties	A cultivar with pretty pink and yellow flowers is occasionally available – expensive but worth searching for

JAPANESE PAINTED FERN
(*Athyrium nipponicum* 'Pictum')

In Victorian times ferns were very popular plants for the shady conservatory and no wonder, for the fronds are a wonderful contrast to other foliage. The Japanese painted fern has typical feathery fronds but with a purple tinge to the green and a silver sheen across the centre.

category	Cool and shady
type	Deciduous fern
flowers	None
leaves	Broad, triangular, divided fronds, sage-green with purple mid-ribs and silver-grey variegation
height	30–45cm (12–18in)
spread	30–45cm (12–18in)
temperature	–5°C (23°F)
position	Shade
planting	13–15cm (5–6in) shallow container or half pot
compost	Equal parts JI No. 2, peat and coarse sand

care	Water freely in spring and summer, only moderately in winter
propagation	Growing ferns from spores is fascinating although it does require a little care (see p.39). Division in mid-spring is recommended
species and varieties	*Nephrolepis exaltata* (sword fern) is usually sold as a houseplant. It has erect, lance-shaped pale green fronds and needs a minimum temperature of 13°C (55°F). The long, strap-like fronds of the hart's-tongue fern, *Asplenium scolopendrium*, are absolutely hardy and there are many interesting cultivars, with crests or ruffled edges. *Asplenium nidus* (bird's nest fern) comes from the tropics. The undivided, broad, pale-green fronds form a rosette with a central well or 'nest'. It needs a warm, humid environment and an acid compost

PITTOSPORUM
(*Pittosporum tobira*)

In the south of France, this neat and well-behaved evergreen is used as a hedging plant, which gives some idea of its adaptability. It always looks tidy and healthy even in drought conditions and in a pot it will stand quite an amount of neglect. It is sometimes known as 'Mock Orange' because of the intense orange-fragrance of its attractive clusters of flowers.

category	Fragrant
type	Evergreen shrub
flowers	Clusters, 8cm (3in) across, of star-shaped creamy-white flowers that fade to yellow.
leaves	Oval, dark green, glossy
height	1.8m (6ft)
spread	2m (6½ft)
temperature	2–7°C (36–45°F)
position	Sunny
planting	23cm (9in) pot
compost	JI No. 2 with some extra sand
care	Easy and good-tempered. Repot when necessary. Water when necessary. Feed each month with balanced fertilizer
propagation	Take 8–10cm (3–4in) semi-ripe cuttings of lateral shoots in summer. Root them with a bottom heat of 16–18°C (61–64°F). When rooted, pot up into 8cm (3in) pots of JI No. 2 and keep frost free over winter
species and varieties	*P. tobira* 'Variegatum' has irregular cream margins to the leaves. There is also a small cultivar, *P. tobira* 'Nanum'

Japanese painted fern

Pittosporum

practical project 1

FERNS FOR THE CONSERVATORY

TROPICAL FERNS

These require a minimum temperature of 10–15°C (50–59°F)

Bird's nest fern *(Asplenium nidus)*
Australian tree fern *(Dicksonia antarctica)*
Sword fern *(Nephrolepis exaltata)*
Nephrolepis exaltata 'Bostoniensis'
Stag's horn fern *(Platycerium bifurcatum)*
Table ferns *Pteris* sp
Selaginella sp

HARDY FERNS

These will flourish in a cold conservatory (see also p.36)

Adiantum pedatum var. *aleuticum*
A. venustum
Asplenium scolopendrium 'Crispum' and other cvs
Athyrium nipponicum 'Pictum'
Fishtail or Holly fern *(Cyrtomium falcatum)*
Shield Fern *(Polystichum setiferum)* and cvs
Liquorice fern *(Polypodium glycyrrhiza)*

For a conservatory that does not get direct sunlight, except perhaps in the early morning, ferns make wonderful decorative plants. They were very popular in Victorian times, when whole glasshouses were dedicated to them. It is easy to understand why: the beauty and variety of their foliage entirely compensates for the fact that they do not flower.

PROVIDING THE RIGHT CONDITIONS

Most ferns require a degree of humidity that may seem to be difficult to provide in a conservatory where there is a lot of wood and upholstered furniture. The fern enthusiast need not be put off, however, as they will grow happily on trays of damp gravel or in double pots insulated with damp sphagnum moss placed between them. (See also p.68.) Alternatively, you can select ferns that do not need such a humid atmosphere.

Two ferns that tolerate drier conditions are the Hare's foot fern, *Davallia canariensis*, and the Button fern, *Pellaea rotundifolia*. The first has a furry creeping rhizome and feathery, carrot-like foliage on wiry stems, while the second has arching fronds about 30cm (12in) long with round leathery leaflets. The

Asparagus fern, *Asparagus setaceus*, which is not a fern at all, makes an attractive contrast to add to a group of these tolerant ferns.

Tropical ferns are often available in small pots from good garden centres. Otherwise there are several specialist growers who will supply plants by mail order (see useful addresses pp.140–1).

MAKING A DISPLAY OF TROPICAL FERNS

YOU WILL NEED

A shady conservatory
Plant pots
Sand
Gravel trays or watertight pots and either gravel or expanded clay granules which absorb moisture or container pots without drainage holes
Peat-based compost
Medium-grade Perlite
Charcoal granules
Balanced powdered fertilizer

- Make a mixture of three parts compost to two parts Perlite. Add 1 cupful of charcoal granules to each litre of the mixture and then add the fertilizer according to the instructions on its packet. Mix well.

- Repot the ferns into 13cm (5in) or 15cm (6in) pots.

- Make a bed of gravel or sand at the bottom. This must be kept permanently moist. Place the plant pots on top. Alternatively, you can group the plant pots together on trays of damp gravel or expanded clay granules. Ensure the pots are standing above the water, not in it, otherwise the roots will rot.

PROPAGATING FERNS FROM SPORES

YOU WILL NEED

A clean sharp knife
Clean white paper
8cm (3¹/₄in) sterile plant pot
Compost
A mister
A fern frond with ripe spore capsules on it

Ferns produce their spores in small capsules on the undersides of the fronds. If ripe these capsules, called sporangia, are plump and often a rust colour.

- Select a suitable frond, cut it off and lay it, face up, on a sheet of white paper. After a day or two the spores, like fine dust, should fall on to the paper.

- Fill a pot with compost and sterilize it further by pouring boiling water over the compost until it runs out of the bottom of the pot. When the compost is cool, shake the spores over the surface, cover the pot with glass or polythene, and then exclude light and put it in a warm place.

- Spray regularly with cool boiled water.

- After one or two weeks the compost should become covered with a green mould. Remove the light excluder. Do not place in direct sunlight or let the compost dry out.

- After a further period small leaves appear; if these are not too crowded, they can be left to develop root systems, otherwise, prick out and replant in small clumps in separate pots. Seedlings will need to be grown on for two more years.

DIVIDING FERNS

Ferns which are too crowded for their pots can be divided and repotted this month. A large rootstock may be cut into four parts. Most aspleniums and athyrium can be divided this way.

- After removing the fern from its pot, shake off loose soil and pull the roots apart.

- If the fern is pot-bound and the roots very dense, you will need to use a sharp knife to divide them.

- Repot each piece into a smaller pot, using fresh JI No. 2 compost.

- Do not water the plant for two or three days to encourage the roots to spread out in search of water. Mist the leaves regularly instead.

- *Asplenium bulbiferum*, the hen and chicken fern, develops plantlets on the edge of the adult leaves. When these have two pairs of leaflets, they can be separated and potted into a small pot filled with a layer of drainage material and a compost of half peat, half sand.

- *Nephrolepis exaltata*, which has several different cultivars, increases rapidly by means of stolons. Separate young plants from the stolons and pot in the same mixture recommended for the asplenium.

AFTERCARE OF YOUR FERN DISPLAY

Both evergreen and deciduous ferns benefit from being kept tidy. Trim off any dead leaves. For deciduous ferns like the Hart's tongue ferns (*Phyllitis scolopendrium* cvs), do this when the new fronds are beginning to uncurl, to give them room to expand. *Nephrolepis* cultivars on the other hand need frequent tidying up throughout the year. Cut just inside the brown areas; avoid damage to healthy tissue.

Make divisions by pulling or cutting

Mist the leaves regularly

Plantlets on the edges of fronds can be removed and potted up

plants
OF THE
month
2

FERNS

BOSTON FERN
(Nephrolepis exaltata 'Bostoniensis'*)*

The Boston fern is a close relation of the Sword fern and is even more popular because of its elegantly arching fronds. These can soon reach 60cm (2ft) and have been known to attain 1.2m (4ft) in mature well grown specimens. Its graceful habit makes this fern ideal for growing in hanging pots and baskets. It is slightly more tolerant of dryness than many ferns.

category	Easy
type	Evergreen fern
leaves	Lance-shaped, divided, pale green
height	30–90cm (1–3ft)
spread	30–90cm (1–3ft)
temperature	10°C (50°F)
position	Good light or shade
planting	15cm (6in) pot. Pot on as necessary. This fern is a fast grower
compost	Acid compost, with added Perlite and charcoal (see project p.38)
care	Water freely in summer and moderately during the winter. Use rain water. Repot every two or three years when mature. Liquid feed every month from spring to autumn in the years between repotting. Remove fading fronds regularly
propagation	Pot up plantlets produced from runners in spring and summer
species and varieties	*N. exaltata* is more erect. *N. exaltata* 'Smithii' and other cultivars have ruffled or feather frond edges

STAG'S HORN FERN
(Platycerium bifurcatum)

An epiphytic fern that grows in trees in the tropical rainforests of Australia. A well grown specimen is absolutely magnificent with leathery grey-green leaves that really do look like a stag's horns. Barren fronds wrap themselves around their support, forming a cylinder that traps debris which rots down forming compost and feeding the plant. The antler-like fronds are fertile and bear spores.

category	Challenging
type	Evergreen fern
leaves	Long leathery fronds forked at the end and covered with fine white hairs
height	1m (3ft)
spread	1m (3ft)

temperature	10°C (50°F)
position	Somewhere with shade from hot sun
planting	Attach a young plant with a cushion of moss and peat compost on to a slab of bark or wood, which needs to be at least 50cm (18in) sq. Use nylon twine to secure it. Hang the specimen high on a wall or pillar for best effect
compost	Peat-based compost with added sphagnum moss
care	The fern must be handled carefully. If the white hairs are damaged, this can cause the frond to shrivel. High humidity is important. Feel into the cylinder of infertile leaves to see if the plant needs watering – it should be damp, but not wet. Give an occasional liquid feed during the summer
propagation	By spores. Occasionally plantlets form and these can be detached and potted on

BIRD'S NEST FERN
(Asplenium nidus)

The glossy lance-shaped fronds of the Bird's nest fern grow out from around a central point, like the feathers of a shuttlecock. The plants have a very luxuriant appearance, the epitome of the tropical rainforest. Make sure, when buying one, that there are tiny curled up leaves in the centre of the 'nest' for this is where any new growth will come from.

category	Challenging
type	Evergreen fern
leaves	Broad, bright green with dark midrib
height	60cm–1.2m (2–4ft)
spread	30–60cm (1–2ft)
temperature	10°C (50°F)
position	Good light but no direct sun
planting	12.5cm (5in) pot. Pot on as necessary
compost	Acid compost, with added Perlite and charcoal (see project p.38)
care	Water freely in summer and moderately during the winter. Use rain water. Give a liquid feed from early summer
propagation	Division in spring, or from spores
species and varieties	*A. bulbiferum*, the Hen and chicken spleenwort, and *A. trichomanes*, the Maidenhair spleenwort, are evergreen ferns from the same family. They are hardy and need quite different treatment

The luxurious green foliage of a group of potted ferns creates an instant tranquil oasis. You could choose a few of these: (left to right) Boston, stag's horn and bird's nest ferns, hen-and-chicken and maidenhair spleenworts

practical project 2

BUILDING A WOODEN POTTING BENCH

The difference between a conservatory and a greenhouse is that the latter is meant to look workmanlike. Bags of potting compost, sprays, packets of fertilizers and tools are usually visible. In a conservatory that is also used as a living space for people, some means of tidying away all these necessary objects has to be found. Even if you don't plan to do any propagation, the plants in the conservatory will need watering, pruning, spraying, top dressing and repotting. Keeping the equipment for all these tasks out in the garage or garden shed is one sure way of putting them off.

One of the messiest jobs in the conservatory is potting and repotting. This month's project is to make a simple wooden potting bench to keep the compost in its place.

A simple sideboard or kitchen unit with drawers and cupboards will hold everything you need, though if you plan to use the top of your storage cupboard as a display space, try to find one with sliding doors which will not be obstructed by trailing plants. Compost keeps better in the plastic bags it is supplied in. Unfortunately these are usually very brightly coloured; not the ideal focal point for a conservatory. You can transfer the compost into other containers, but these must be airtight, to keep the compost moist. Small plastic dustbins with tightly fitting lids are ideal if they can found in quiet colours like brown or dull green. Otherwise, compost bags need to be kept discreetly out of sight in a cupboard. Sprayers and bags of sand and gravel also need cupboard space. Other equipment like secateurs, dibbers, string and seed packets can be kept in drawers. Chests and storage benches have the dis-

advantage that their flat tops too easily become additional display space for plants. Then it is difficult to lift the lid and get inside. A window seat with sliding door cupboard underneath is worth considering for those who can bend easily.

The potting bench is 76cm (30in) wide by the depth of the surface you have available (Xcm/Xin) and 23cm (9in) high. The bottom, sides and back are cut from the plywood and the frame from the batten.

■ For the sides, cut two pieces of plywood 23cm (9in) by Xcm/in.

■ Use the compasses to draw a curve at one end of each piece, setting them to 17cm (6³/₄in). The arc should touch front and top edges and both pieces must be identical.

YOU WILL NEED

Imperial measurements given are not exact conversions but are the equivalents as used by most hardware stores selling wood

5.5mm (¹/₄in) thick plywood
21 x 21mm (⁷/₈ x ⁷/₈in) batten
(For a potting bench 60cm (24in) deep, you will need a piece of plywood 120cm x 90cm (48 x 36in) and 308cm (10ft 2in) of batten)
Compasses
Saw, Wood glue, Panel pins
Non-toxic wood preservative (or polyurethane varnish)
Wood stain (if preferred)

- For the back cut a piece of plywood 76cm (30in) by 23cm (9in).

- For the bottom (which will form the floor of the potting bench) cut a piece of plywood 76cm (30in) by Xcm/in.

- Cut two cross battens 76cm (30in) long and two side battens of Xcm minus 5cm (2in) and two back battens 23cm (9in) long.

- Fasten cross and side battens to the bottom piece with glue and panel pins.

- Fasten the back to the back battens in the same way.

- Then join the back to the rear cross batten.

- Finally pin and glue the sides to side and back battens.

- Sand any rough visible edges.

- Finish by painting with non-toxic preservative, wood stain and/or polyurethane varnish.

APRIL

With a little forward planning the conservatory in mid-spring can be an Aladdin's cave of brilliant colour, for this is the month when autumn-sown annuals burst into flower. Clarkia *is an old garden favourite that makes a good pot plant at this time of year . C. concinna 'Pink Ribbons' is very eye-catching as is C. breweri with its interesting, spidery petals. This is the time to think ahead and save a few seeds from the packets of hardy annuals you are just about to sow outside.*

Many of the winter- and spring-flowering shrubs and perennials are still in bloom. Late camellias and Coronilla glauca *(the variegated version is colourful all year) have been joined by the Australian mint bush,* Prostanthera rotundifolia *and the parrot's beak or lobster claw,* Clianthus puniceus *with its strange beaked flowers of terracotta red.*

Winter-flowering begonias and early blooming kalanchoes are accompanied now by ranunculus and Nemophila menzesii 'Snowstorm'. *In a heated conservatory cannas and clivias, zantedeschias and forced hydrangeas create a lush tropical effect. Amongst all the tropical splendour and vivid hues do not overlook the more modest plants or those whose leaves are their main attraction. Violets, ferns, bamboos and cissus provide easy to grow valuable quiet contrasts to the dramatic and exotic. Strange tufted shoots of bamboo appear as if by magic, delicate Parma violets nestle among their heart-shaped leaves while the curled fronds of ferns uncoil in a leisurely way.*

The weather out-of-doors is still very variable but indoors pests are multiplying in the sheltered surroundings. Many plants will need weak liquid feeds. Well, but not over-fed, plants are less vulnerable to pests and diseases. At midday on sunny days, a conservatory facing full sun can overheat. A daily inspection this month is necessary to keep an eye on all the activity. Luckily, with so many plants at their best, this is a pleasure not a chore.

tasks
FOR THE
month

ROUTINE TASKS

Continue to hand pollinate the flowers of strawberries, peaches and nectarines (p.103). Begin to give them regular liquid feeds

Increase frequency of liquid feed to other plants as they grow more quickly

Make sure vulnerable plants and seedlings are in shade at midday

Sow seeds of asparagus fern, coleus and torenia for the summer display and sow seeds of cineraria for winter flowering

There may still be frosts in cooler areas. Keep an eye on the weather forecasts

Ventilate the conservatory regularly every day but close it up carefully at night

CHECKLIST

- Keep plants clean and tidy
- Identify plant disorders
- Treat pests and diseases

PLANT MAINTENANCE

The weather should be beginning to warm up but even if it is not, the plants will be responding to longer hours of daylight and be in vigorous growth.

Make your plants look their best by removing dead and disfigured leaves and by washing any dust from leaves, with a spray or sponge. Smooth-leaved plants can be wiped with a damp lint-free cloth. Many plants can be put outside on a showery day to freshen their foliage but be sure to bring them in again before mid-afternoon. Plants that are looking weak or leggy can be cut hard back. Trailing plants can have their growing tips pinched out, to make them bushier.

PLANT DISORDERS

Not all plant failures, however, are caused by pests or diseases. Sometimes they are protesting about the management when they drop their leaves! The most common disorders are listed below, together with suggested treatments.

TREATING PESTS AND DISEASES

Plants may be in vigorous growth, but so, unfortunately, are pests and fungi as the sheltered atmosphere of a conservatory suits them very well. Good hygiene and management will help to protect the conservatory against some pests and diseases and perhaps the best way of preventing an infestation is by regular vigilance and routine examination. The first unwelcome guests can then be destroyed manually or very simply. If pests go unnoticed for a week or two, however, it becomes very difficult to eradicate them without the use of insecticides, fungicides and other chemicals. The most common pests and diseases are listed opposite, together with suggested treatments.

Many chemicals are being withdrawn from sale and will not be available for amateurs in the future. The names of chemicals given below are **not** the names of the products that contain them. You will need to **read carefully the labels** of proprietary products to make sure that you get a pesticide containing the appropriate chemical.

PLANT DISORDERS

Symptoms	Cause	Treatment
New leaves turn yellow	Lack of iron	Water with rainwater; apply a chelated form of trace elements and sequestered iron
Oldest leaves turn yellow	Temperature too low	Move plants from draughts or away from exposed positions; check on temperature levels
Leaves turn slowly yellow then fall	Too much water	Reduce watering and allow soil or compost to dry out between waterings
Pale yellow leaves all over plant	Lack of nitrogen	Apply a high nitrogen fertilizer such as sulphate of ammonia
Older leaves are yellow but have green veins	Lack of magnesium	Apply Epsom salts either to the soil or as a foliar feed
Brown edges and tips of leaves	Atmosphere too dry; compost and water too alkaline; lack of potassium	Increase humidity (see p.68); in hard-water areas use cool boiled water, rainwater or melted ice from a defrosted fridge
Brown patches and blotches on leaves	Sun scorching	Provide shelter from the sun, particularly when it is at its hottest
Puckered and distorted leaves	Irregular watering	Water more regularly and more generously, especially during hot spells
Buds and flowers drop	Atmosphere or compost is too dry; plants may have been moved or experienced sudden changes of temperature; red spider mites may be present	Increase humidity (see p.68) and water more carefully; avoid moving plants, especially in winter; for treatment of red spider mite see main chart

PESTS AND DISEASES

Pest	Damage	Method of Control	
ANTS (building nests in pots)	Plant roots are damaged and the plant may wilt	Water the compost and the base of the conservatory walls with HCH, permethrin or pirimiphos-methyl	1
APHIDS (1)	Plants are weakened by these sap-sucking insects	Humidity and ventilation keeps numbers down; small infestations can be squashed; bring in some ladybirds; attract predatory hoverflies by growing Tagetes patula (French marigold); use organic pesticides like derris or pyrethrum	
LEAFMINER (2) (particularly chrysanthemums and cinerarias)	Whitish brown trails appear within the leaf structure	Destroy affected leaves and spray with dimethoate, HCH or pirimiphos-methyl	
RED SPIDER MITE	Grey or yellowish mottling on leaves; very fine webs on plants	Increase humidity by spraying shelves and floor with water, also spray undersides of leaves of affected plants; use the predator Phytoseiulus persimilis in the early stages of attack if your conservatory has daytime temperatures of at least 21°C (70°F); derris, malathion and pirimiphos-methyl may help	2
			3
SCALE INSECTS (3) (particularly citrus and bay trees)	Flat brown, grey or white, rounded scales on the undersides of leaves	The parasitic wasp Metaphycus helvolus will control numbers; touch each scale with a brush dipped in methylated spirits then scrape it off; use malathion or pirimiphos-methyl	
THRIPS (4) (particularly achimenes, cyclamen, primula, sinningia, saintpaulia, streptocarpus)	White flecks on flower petals	Increase humidity (see red spider mites); spray with dimethoate, malathion, permethrin or pirimiphos-methyl; try predatory mites Amblyseius spp.	4
TORTRIX MOTH (5)	Leaves are rolled up and may contain green caterpillars, and the undersides of the leaves are eaten, leaving brown patches	Squash the rolled up leaves; spray with permethrin or pirimiphos-methyl; phemerone traps work with Cacoecimorpha pronubana, one tortrix species	
VINE WEEVIL	Plants grow slowly then wilt and die and stems below ground are eaten; fat white larvae, with brown heads, are found in the compost	Biological control is in the form of nematodes which are watered in; or soak the pots with HCH or pirimiphos-methyl	
WHITEFLY (6) (particularly brugmansias, buddleias, cinerarias, fuchsias, lantanas, pelargoniums)	Clouds of flies fly up from leaves when they are disturbed	Use soft soap spray early in the season and put up yellow sticky traps, then when the weather is warmer use a parasitic wasp, Encarsia formosa, released at regular intervals; growing pots of mint may help	5
WOODLICE	Roots and seedlings eaten	Maintain high standards of cleanliness, remove any dead plant material; protect seedlings with HCH dust; boiling water is brutal but effective	
Disease	**Damage**	**Method of Control**	6
BOTRYTIS OR GREY MOULD (7)	Furry grey growth on leaves spreads to the rest of the plant	Improve ventilation, spread your pot plants out to improve air circulation; remove and destroy affected plants; spray with a proprietary fungicide	
SOOTY MOULD	Black sticky patches on leaves, often after infestation of scale insects, aphids or whiteflies – these secrete sticky substances which are then colonized by moulds	Glossy leaves can be wiped clean; the best treatment is to get rid of the pests (see above)	7
POWDERY MILDEW (8) (particularly on pot-grown roses)	White powdery growth on leaves and plants	Pick off and destroy affected leaves; spray both sides of the leaves with sulphur or a proprietary fungicide	
DAMPING-OFF	Seedlings keel over and their roots rot off	Avoid overcrowding seedlings, overwatering and too much humidity; water newly planted seeds with Cheshunt compound	8

plants
OF THE
month

KANGAROO VINE
(*Cissus antarctica*)

The kangaroo vine, best known and easily available as a houseplant, makes an excellent foliage climber for a shady wall. Each leaf has a tiny tendril growing opposite to it which helps the plant to hoist itself up.

category	Cool and shady
type	Evergreen climber
flowers	Not important
leaves	Rich green, slightly leathery; a pointed oval in shape with serrated edges
height	4.5m (15ft)
spread	3–4.5m (10–15ft)

temperature	7°C (45°F)
position	Shade
planting	20cm (8in) pot to restrict size. Best planted in the border if required to cover a whole wall, roof beam or pillar
compost	JI No. 2 with added peat and sand
care	Well-drained compost is essential. Water heavily but allow to dry out between waterings. Weak liquid feed when plant is in full growth. Pinch out growing tips regularly so that plant branches out
propagation	Take 5cm (2in) shoots with a heel in spring or summer and insert these in sand or a very sandy compost in a propagator with bottom heat and good humidity
species and varieties	*C. rhombifolia* (grape ivy) is more delicate in appearance and the leaves grow in threes

VIOLET
(*Viola odorata*)

Although this plant, and its pink sister, *V. o. rosea*, are completely hardy, the delicate but unmistakable perfume can be appreciated more fully when they are grown in pots indoors. They flower earlier too.

category	Fragrant
type	Semi-evergreen perennial
flowers	Violet, white or pink, small, fragrant on long stems
leaves	Heart-shaped
height	7cm (3in)
spread	15cm (6in)
temperature	Fully hardy
position	Shady
planting	8cm (3in) pot
compost	Moisture retentive. JI No. 2 with added peat
care	Mist foliage and flowers in warm weather. Keep the plants cool as they stop producing flower buds as soon as they get too warm. Feed every three weeks throughout year with a balanced fertilizer
propagation	Divide off any runners and pot them up separately
species and varieties	If you can find any of the Parma violets that the Victorians loved, and a few nurseries still have them, snap them up. Cultivars to look for are *V.* 'Duchesse de Parme', *V.* 'Marie Louise', *V.* 'Comte de Brazza' and *V.* 'Parme de Toulouse'

BAMBOO
(Phyllostachys nigra)

This elegant, black-stemmed bamboo creates a wonderful oriental effect in a conservatory. The slender shoots, which are green when young, arch gracefully and the narrow leaves grow in feathery masses. Enhance the eastern effect by planting it in a glazed ceramic pot.

category	Easy
type	Evergreen, clump-forming bamboo
flowers	Unimportant
leaves	The narrow leaves, 7–10cm (3–4in) long, hang in heavy clusters
height	1.8–2.5cm (6–8ft)
spread	Restricted in pot
temperature	–3–7°C (27–45°F)
position	Good light with some sun
planting	Large pot
compost	JI No. 2
care	Water well in summer but only sparingly in winter. Liquid feed during the summer
propagation	Divide and replant in mid-spring
species and varieties	*Pleioblastus auricomus* is much smaller and very colourful with green and yellow striped leaves and purple stems. *Nandina domestica* 'Firepower' (heavenly bamboo, sacred bamboo) changes colour in the autumn, from light green to crimson. It has white flowers followed by red berries and is less hardy than the others mentioned

BRUNFELSIA
(Brunfelsia pauciflora)

The 'yesterday, today and tomorrow' plant is also known as 'morning, noon and night' because of its habit of changing its flower colour. The flowers start as an intense purple-blue, change to lavender and then fade to near-white.

category	Challenging
type	Evergreen shrub
flowers	5cm (2in) wide, flat, with five petals
leaves	Long, lanceolate and a glossy light green
height	75–150cm (30–60in)
spread	75–150cm (30–60in)
temperature	16–30°C (60–85°F) for flowering. They will survive at 10°C (50°F)
position	Full sun in winter and partial shade in summer
planting	Keep the plant in a pot to restrict growth
compost	Ericaceous compost
care	Feed well during the summer but stop in autumn. Brunfelsias have a tendency to chlorosis and if the leaves go yellow, it will need dosing with a plant tonic containing iron, such as Sequestrene or Miracid. If the temperature falls, they drop their leaves. They are also sensitive to fumes from gas. They need to be kept in a warm and humid atmosphere. Prune lightly after flowering, removing stem tips to maintain a compact shape. Repot only when roots fill container
propagation	Take 8cm (3in) tip cuttings in spring or summer. Insert four in a mixture of coarse sand and peat in a 9cm (3¹/₂in) pot and root at a temperature of 21°C (70°F)
species and varieties	*B. pauciflora* 'Macrantha' has larger flowers. *B. americana* has scented white flowers

practical project 1

PLANNING EFFECTIVE VENTILATION

Ventilation becomes even more important from now on. Plants in the open garden are growing in moving air, even on what appears to be a completely still day. Air movement in the conservatory keeps plants healthy and lowers temperatures. There are a number of methods of encouraging movement of air. The simplest, of course, is to open doors and windows, but this may not always be possible for security reasons. Old greenhouses were ventilated by a combination of rooflights and low-level air vents; with constant attention, these devices worked very well. However, nowadays when many people are out at work, automatic vent openers and ventilation fans are the ideal solutions to the problem of trapped hot air. Colonial-type ceiling fans give a wonderful period atmosphere to a conservatory with a high roof, and work well too, but they have to be used in conjunction with good shading.

There are three sorts of rooflight openers: the manual (you), the non-electric and the electric.

Non-electric

The non-electric rooflight opener is operated by an ingenious tube full of wax. The wax expands as the temperature increases, pushing a spring that lifts the rooflight open. The temperature has to be quite high (over 16°C/61°F) before these start opening so they cannot be used for ensuring fresh air in the winter. (Necessary if you are growing chrysanthemums, peaches and vines – all of which need a cool climate, with good ventilation, until quite late in the year.) Non-electric louvre openers that work on the same

principle as the rooflight opener are also available. You need to have some idea of the weight of your rooflight to choose the right size of opener.

Electric

Electrical vent motors are much more expensive but are particularly effective for heavy, double-glazed rooflights. They work on a hydraulic ram principle and some operate more than one window at a time.

Fans

A window- or wall-mounted ventilation fan, placed high up and working in conjunction with low-level vents or louvres, can also be very effective in creating changes of air and reducing temperatures. Both types can be thermostatically controlled.

An extractor fan should be installed opposite the door, near the apex of the facing wall. For conservatories of up to 8m³ (280ft³) a 20cm (7½in) diameter fan is necessary; for 8–14m³ (280–500ft³), a 25cm (9in) fan, and for 14–28m³ (500–1,000ft³), a 30cm (12in) fan. The fan can be fixed into a panel of resin-bonded plywood, cut to match the pane of glass it will replace. Check that it has automatic shutters to prevent draughts coming into the conservatory.

All of these different systems come with full instructions for installation and the necessary fittings. Good DIY stores, garden centres and garden shops should have more than one type. Gardening magazines carry advertisements for many different fans, heaters and automatic vent openers.

FITTING A SIMPLE AUTOMATIC SYSTEM

YOU WILL NEED

Automatic louvre opener
Automatic vent opener
Drill with 3mm (⅛in) bit (for louvre opener)
Additional 6mm (³/₁₆in) bit (for fitting automatic vent opener to aluminium bars)
File
Screwdriver
Thermometer (to check conservatory temperature)
Pencil or ballpoint pen
Tape measure

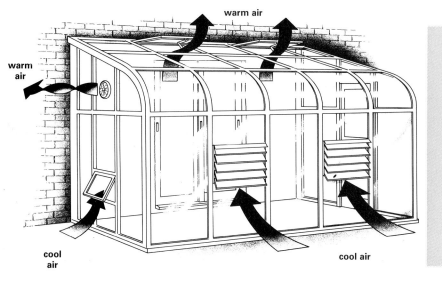

warm air

warm air

cool air

cool air

Two automatic openers, one fitted to a low-level louvre window and another to a rooflight, are the simplest, trouble-free way of providing adequate ventilation. If you do not have low-level louvres, a kit that fits all greenhouses and re-uses the original glass is inexpensive and available by mail order. It consists of the side operating components for a 5-bladed louvre. It is supplied with fixing bolts for an aluminium conservatory but it can easily be fitted to wooden frames with wood screws.

AUTOMATIC LOUVRE OPENER

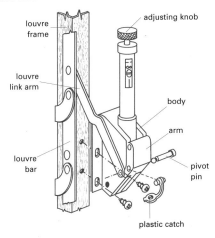

Installing the automatic louvre opener
■ Remove the handle on the louvre windows by either drilling or filing the rivets. Then remove the screw that holds the louvre link arm to the handle (Fig 1).

MANUAL LOUVRE OPENER

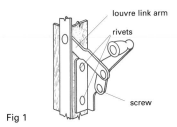

Fig 1

■ Check that the louvre still moves freely. Adjust it if necessary and lubricate all moving parts.
■ On the automatic opener, insert the pivot pin through the arm (Fig 2).
■ Push on the plastic catch and then fit the link arm, which is on the louvre frame, over the catch and push on the top half of the catch (Fig 3 and 4).
■ Place the louvre control unit against the louvre frame and push on the body so that the louvre link arm is fully closed and the unit is flush and square.
■ Mark the position for the screw holes on the frame.
■ Drill two holes 3mm ($\frac{1}{8}$in) diameter. Then loosely screw the unit in. Push upwards until the louvre link arm is tightly closed and then tighten the screws.
■ Set the temperature at which the automatic opener will start to work. This is done by screwing the adjusting knob on the louvre control unit clockwise until it is tight when the temperature in the conservatory is about 16°C (61°F). As soon as the temperature rises above this, the louvres will start to open.

Installing the vent opener
The automatic roof vent opener should be kept in a refrigerator or other cool place for 30 minutes before fixing. This ensures that the wax in it is cool. When it is cool enough, you should be able to feel a springy resistance when you push the piston into the tube.

The design and material of rooflights varies; they may have deep or shallow sill bars, and can be made of wood and aluminium. Each design needs a slightly different method of fixing. The important thing to remember is to centre the vent opener carefully on the rooflight and the frame.

Aluminium-framed rooflight For an aluminium-framed rooflight, it is safer to remove the bottom rail and sill when drilling the holes for the screws. Make these 5mm ($\frac{3}{16}$in) in diameter for the 4 screws which are provided with the opener. For a roof vent with a deep sill bar, secure the bottom rail T-bracket to the underside of the bottom rail. Then fix the sill bar T-bracket to the face of the sill bar.

Wooden-framed rooflight For a wooden-framed rooflight with a deep sill bar, use 4 wood screws and 2 round headed screws provided. Secure the bottom rail T-bracket to the underside of the bottom rail and secure the sill T-bracket to the face of the sill.

To set the unit Wait until the temperature is steady at about 16°C (61°F). Take the hexagon adjuster and slip it over the piston rod. Lift the vent about 15cm (6in) and screw the adjuster into the swivelling block until it holds the vent slightly open when you take your hand away.

Fig 2

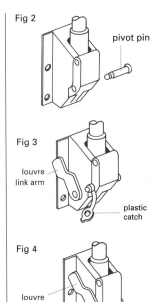

pivot pin

Fig 3

louvre link arm

plastic catch

Fig 4

louvre link arm

AUTOMATIC ROOFLIGHT OPENER FITTED TO AN ALUMINIUM ROOFLIGHT

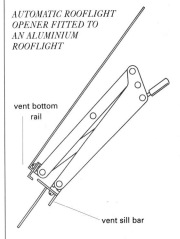

vent bottom rail

vent sill bar

AUTOMATIC ROOFLIGHT OPENER FITTED TO A WOODEN ROOFLIGHT

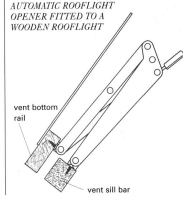

vent bottom rail

vent sill bar

practical project 2

A 'TREE' FOR BROMELIADS

Ananas bracteatus 'Tricolor'

Tillandsia, or 'airplants', are widely available in many different species. These fascinating plants can be grown in a warm conservatory, or in the house. They look very effective displayed on pieces of bark or a 'tree' made from a dead branch. Other epiphytic plants, like bromeliads and some cacti, can also be grown this way, as they do in the tropical and semi-tropical rainforest. The pieces of bark or the tree branch may be quite small, or as large as you have room for.

Epiphytes use their roots to cling on to a surface, but they get their nourishment from the atmosphere which, in their natural habitat, is mist and low cloud. In the home or conservatory, they must be misted regularly and it may be difficult to grow them where the atmosphere has to remain dry for other plants, or for furnishings. However, many of the epiphytes are very beautiful and if the heat in which they will flourish can be provided, they can easily become a passion which will outstrip your worries about furnishings or the health of chrysanthemums.

●
MAKING THE TREE

YOU WILL NEED

A suitable branch
Horticultural timber preservative
Horticultural adhesive
Wire (fine copper or plastic-coated) or nylon twine
Live sphagnum moss
A selection of epiphytic plants
If you are making your tree in a pot you will also need:
Cement, Sand or Ready-mixed sand and cement
Stones, or other ballast
A large pot

■ If you have a soil bed, then the branch can be inserted deeply into the soil. Otherwise, a large, firmly-based pot can be used and stones and mortar packed around the branch to keep it stable.

■ First, you must treat that part of the 'tree' that will be embedded either in soil or in mortar with a timber preservative so it does not rot.

WARNING

■ *Choose a preservative that will not harm living plants or the soil. Follow the instructions on the can. Do not use ordinary creosote.* ■

■ In the border, dig a hole that is at least 45cm (18in) deep, place the treated branch in it and use some large stones to wedge the branch tightly in position before refilling the hole with soil and pressing it very firmly down.

■ In the pot, wedge the branch with stones and fill the spaces with mortar: buy ready-mixed sand and cement to save time.

■ **Important** If you wish to set the branch at a picturesque angle, ensure that the weight of the pot when filled with stones and cement is sufficient to support both the 'tree' and the mature plants that will be on it.

■ Before positioning them on the 'tree', remove most of the soil from around the roots of epiphytic orchids, ferns and bromeliads and replace it with live sphagnum moss.

■ Then wedge the plants in the angles between branches or attach them to the branch and fasten them with suitable fine nylon twine or copper wire.

■ Tillandsias need no moss and should be attached with special adhesive towards the top of the 'tree' so that drips from other plants do not fall on them.

■ When decorating your 'tree' take account of the habit of the plants and their likely size at maturity.

■ Check the design for balance. Contrasts of texture and leaf size are good, but avoid making too many otherwise the result will look bitty.

■ At first the plants, which are usually best 'planted' when they are quite small, will look insignificant, and the tree bare. One way of overcoming this is to buy more than one plant of each species. Group them together, but fix the additional ones on to a piece of bark which can be removed entirely as the plants grow larger. (It can be used for another display in the house.)

Large 'tree' secured in conservatory border

AFTERCARE

■ *The 'tree' and its plants should be misted daily with soft water or rainwater. Keep the sphagnum moss around the roots moist as well as misting the leaves. In spring and summer add proprietary pot plant fertilizer, at ¹/₄ strength, once a month.* ■

SUGGESTED PLANTS

Spanish moss *Tillandsia usneoides* – hangs from branches in a tangle of silvery thread-like stems covered with tiny grey scale-like leaves

Tillandsia cyanea – very different in shape from Spanish moss, with a rosette of narrow, dark green leaves. The flower stem is short and the violet-blue flowers emerge from a paddle-shaped arrangement of pink-tinged, green bracts. Ht 20cm (9in). Sp 30cm (12in)

Flaming sword *Vriesia splendens* – rosette of dark green leaves, horizontally striped with purple-black. The flower, which rises to 60cm (24in), is a spike of vivid red bracts and yellow flowers. Ht and Sp 30cm (12in)

Bird's nest fern *Asplenium nidus* – rosette of broad, bright green fronds. It will grow in a pot and is sometimes cheaply available as a very small plant. Ht 60–120cm (24–48in). Sp 30-60cm (12–24in)

Urn plant *Aechmea fasciata* – rosette of grey-green broad leaves, horizontally banded with silver. The flowering spike consists of pyramids of blue flowers amid bright pink bracts. Ht 40–60cm (16–24in). Sp 30–50cm (12–20in)

Small 'tree' fitted into a pot

Vriesia splendens

Aechmea fasciata

MAY

This is the beginning of the season when high temperatures and not low ones are the conservatory gardener's problem. Good ventilation is very important from now on and so also is shading. Unless the conservatory is already in deep shade it will need shading in some way. Owners of new conservatories can find themselves looking at a very bright, arid space this month and feel impelled to fill it quickly. But beware: this is the optimum season for garden companies to sell their products.

It is not necessary to buy expensive blinds and plants to make the conservatory a pleasant place to be in its first season. Shade it simply with home-made blinds or use shading paint. Unless you are experienced at growing plants under glass in different conditions, start with the simplest ones and proceed slowly. Pelargoniums of all types can be relied on (and can be stored in the spare bedroom during cold weather) while many shrubs that are almost *hardy* out-of-doors in your area, will give you much anxiety-free pleasure in a pot in the conservatory.

You may not have been able to pot the bulbs of Lilium longiflorum which are a feature of the conservatory this month, but you may be able to buy some potted lilies already in flower. You can also still plant quick-growing French beans or melon seeds in growbags to give an instant indoor garden effect. This is just the right month for planting up some hanging baskets too.

This is the month of the flower shows. At the big shows, specialist nurseries, experts in particular plant families, will display the very best plants they have. There will be early bulbs that have been kept cool to delay flowering and herbaceous perennials that have been forced into flower early. Nurserymen specializing in rare bromeliads, orchids, ferns, pelargoniums and even passion flowers will be available to discuss their finer points. What better places to discover new plants for the conservatory or how to grow the ones you already have?

tasks
FOR THE
month

ROUTINE TASKS

Pinch out the growing tips of fuchsias if they are 10–13cm (4–5in) high

Ventilate freely using the rooflight to avoid draughts. If the weather is warm enough, ventilate at night as well

Make sure that there is some shade at midday

Water daily

Watch out for pests

If there are signs of whitefly, it should be warm enough to release the biological predator *Encarsia formosa* into the conservatory

If you are sowing seeds of biennials like wallflowers and stocks this month, remember that a few plants of each of these could be potted up in early autumn to provide fragrant flowers for the conservatory in spring

CHECKLIST

- Care for bulbs after flowering
- Caring for winter-flowering shrubs
- Grow fruit
- Plant up hanging baskets

BULB AFTERCARE

Remove all dead flowers from bulbs. Allow the leaves to die back naturally, continuing to water slightly. Move pots outside, or alternatively, heel the bulbs into the garden.

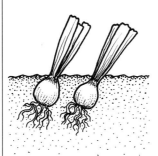

Nerines, freesias and lachenalias can be baked on a shelf near the glass to ripen the bulbs. Arum lilies also need to be rested, and pots of arums should be laid on their side under the bench, or other out of the way place, and not watered again until the end of summer. The same treatment is necessary for mature cyclamen.

CARING FOR WINTER-FLOWERING SHRUBS

Once shrubs in pots have finished blooming they will benefit from being moved outside at the end of the month until mid-autumn.
   Camellias and azaleas should be placed in a shady spot and watered and fed

regularly. Citrus plants can stand in full sun. Roses will be best in part-shade.

FRUIT GROWING

You should have your first taste of summer this month as strawberries grown in the conservatory will be ready to pick. The first bunch of grapes is still to come, however. Tie in new vine growths now and pinch back shoots. Stop vine laterals by pinching out the growing point one leaf beyond the second bunch of grapes. (See also p.102.)
   It may already be necessary to thin the fruits on peaches, nectarines and apricots. When the fruits are the size of a thumbnail, reduce them to one fruit per cluster. Later, they will have to be thinned to one fruit for every 15–22cm (6–9in) of branch for peaches and nectarines, and one fruit per 8cm (3in) for apricots.
   Fan-trained trees should have shoots that are growing directly outwards, or towards the wall or downwards, pruned away. Young side shoots that overlap adjoining branches should be pinched back to four or six leaves.
   The growing point of a melon should be pinched out when the main shoot is 2m (6¹⁄₂ft) long. This will encourage the development of lateral shoots. Pinch out the tips of laterals when they have five leaves. Sub-lateral shoots should then be pinched out two leaves beyond any flower.

PLANTING UP HANGING BASKETS

Well-filled and well-grown hanging baskets may be permanent occupants of the conservatory or just seasonal additions.
   Late spring is the time to plant a summer basket. The inexpensive 'baby' plants that are available at garden centres are ideal for the purpose as they are much easier to plant through the mesh of the basket and the material lining it. None of the artificial liners have quite the natural appeal of moss but new products are being developed all the time and it is well worth experimenting. The secret of success is to have at hand twice as many plants as you think you will need and be generous with them.

■ Collect together your basket, liner, the plants, good compost and a bucket or large pot on which to support the basket. Water-retentive granules and slow-release fertilizer can be mixed with the compost at this stage.

■ Line the basket with moss (3cm (1¹⁄₄in) thick), or other material, and add some handfuls of compost.

■ Carefully insert the first layer of plants through the mesh into the compost. A cone of paper round the plants will protect them as you do this.

■ Add more compost and firm the roots in.

■ Add a further layer of moss and compost and another batch of plants. Do this once more.

■ The remaining plants should be planted in the top of the basket. Choose an upright plant for the centre and trailing plants to grow over the edge.

■ Leave a slight depression in the surface of the compost to aid watering. Keep well-watered and well-fed all season.

For permanent baskets on display for most of the year, one single, large plant can be highly effective and is easier to manage. A water-retentive basket liner can be used. Arching plants like *Nephrolepis exaltata* (see Plants of the Month p.40), the Christmas cactus, *Schlumbergera bridgesii*, fuchsias and, for the expert, some of the epiphytic orchids, look graceful growing in a hanging basket. Trailing plants such as the columneas, *Lotus berthelotii, Ceropegia linearis* ssp. *woodii, Hoya lanceolata* ssp. *bella* and *Begonia sutherlandii* create a luxuriant effect cascading from suspended baskets or pots.

A loam-based compost like JI No, 2 is suitable for the permanent baskets. Daily watering and regular liquid feeding will be necessary. Keep the plants tidy and compact by dead heading, trimming trailing plants that have become too long, and thinning out any tangles.

PLANTS FOR HANGING BASKETS

Aporocactus flagelliformis (Rat's-tail cactus)
Begonia sutherlandii
Tuberous begonia hybrids
Campanula isophylla
Ceropegia linearis subsp. **woodii**
Chlorophytum comosum
Columnea ssp.
Fuchsia spp, trailing or compact upright
Hoya bella
Kalanchoe manginii
Kalanchoe 'Tessa', and other cvs
Lotus berthelotii
Pelargoniums
Schlumbergera bridgesii
Sedum morganianum
Senecio rowleyanus (String-of-beads)

Line the basket with moss and some compost

Carefully insert the first layer of plants

Finally plant up the top of the basket

plants
OF THE
month
1

 ## ANGEL PELARGONIUM
(Pelargonium 'Kettle Baston'*)*

Almost all the pelargoniums are wonderful plants for a sunny conservatory and selecting one from among the hundreds available is very much a matter of personal choice. The 'angel pelargoniums' are small, long-flowering versions of regal pelargoniums and have delicate bicoloured flowers in shades ranging from white to deep red and rich purple. *P.* 'Kettle Baston' has an Award of Garden Merit from the Royal Horticultural Society.

category	Easy
type	Evergreen perennial
flowers	Royal purple top petals and mauve-pink lower petals
leaves	Light green, rounded with three lobes and serrated edges
height	30–90cm (12–36in)
spread	30cm (12in)
temperature	3°C (37°F)
position	Sunny
planting	10–15cm (4–6in) pots
compost	JI No. 2
care	Repot or pot on pelargoniums in early spring. Water well while in growth. Feed with a weak liquid feed at ten day intervals from late spring to early autumn. In the winter protect from frost and keep the plants just moist
propagation	Take 8cm (3in) cuttings in late summer, using a sharp knife to cut the stems at a node. Root in individual 9cm (3½in) pots of cutting compost. Do not cover the cuttings but keep them shaded. Pinch out the growing tips when the cuttings are 15cm (6in) high
species and varieties	*P.* 'Aztec' is a regal pelargonium with rounded, serrated leaves on a plant that can reach 60cm (24in) high and more across. It has bright red flowers veined with purple and with white margins. *P.* 'La France' is an ivy-leaved pelargonium, with double mauve flowers flecked with maroon. Its trailing habit makes it an ideal subject for hanging baskets. The scented-leaved pelargoniums have attractive foliage while the leaves of some of the zonal varieties can be as vivid as the flowers

MARANTA
(Maranta leuconeura 'Erythroneura'*)*

The marantas come from tropical Brazil and need a still, warm, humid atmosphere in which to flourish. They are widely available as pot plants but the atmosphere of a conservatory suits them much better than a windowsill. This cultivar is a striking foliage plant with red veins that make a dramatic fishbone pattern on each leaf. The leaves stand upright at night but are flat during the day. White or mauve flowers may be produced but are not showy.

category	Challenging
type	Evergreen perennial
leaves	15cm (6in) oblong; red veins on a background of dark green with an irregular paler strip down the centre
height	30cm (12in)
spread	30cm (12in)
temperature	10–15°C (50–59°F)
position	Shade from hot sun
planting	They are rapid growers and will need potting on several times. Finish in 13–15cm (5–6in) pots or 15–20cm (6–8in) pans
compost	Equal parts JI No. 2 and all-purpose, peat-based compost
care	Repot established plants in spring each year and liquid feed every two weeks from late spring to early autumn. Marantas must have a humid atmosphere. Water well from early spring to early autumn and mist daily with rainwater in hot weather and while the plant is in full growth. Avoid draughts
propagation	Divide and replant rhizomatous roots in mid-spring or, from late spring to late summer, take cuttings of basal shoots with two or three leaves attached. Root them in cutting compost in a propagator at 21°C (70°F)
species and varieties	*M. leuconeura* var. *kerchoviana* has dark green blotches on the leaves that look like the marks of rabbits' feet running down the plant

EASTER LILY
(Lilium longiflorum)

The beautiful but tender *L. longiflorum* is perfect for growing in a pot or tub in a cool conservatory where it will flower as early as late spring. It is known as the Easter lily or the

Bermuda lily and is often grown commercially as a cut flower because it is ideal for forcing.

category	Fragrant
type	Bulb
flowers	A cluster of from one to six, long, funnel-shaped pure white blooms; very fragrant
leaves	Lance-shaped, 8–13cm (3–5in) long and scattered
height	To 90cm (36in)
temperature	8°C (46°F) should be maintained to produce early growth
position	Full sun but put in the shade in summer after flowering
planting	Plant the bulbs in autumn if possible, in a clay pot at least 30cm (12in) deep. The bottom of the pot should have a layer of crocks, gravel or other drainage material. Follow this with a layer of leafmould or well-rotted manure. Then add the compost and plant the lilies half-way down the container. Cover them with 5–8cm (2–3in) of compost. Three bulbs to a large pot look effective
compost	JI No. 2 with some extra grit. *L. longiflorum* is lime-tolerant
care	Ventilation of the conservatory is important to avoid high temperatures (above 32°C/90°F). Use a systemic insecticide such as permethrin against aphids before they appear
propagation	*L. longiflorum* produces bulblets which appear above the bulb at the base of the stem. These can be detached and planted about 2.5cm (1in) apart in pots. Press the bulblets into any good compost and cover them with a layer of grit. Keep them under the bench in the conservatory or in a frame; do not let them dry out and be patient. They take several years to reach flowering size. Lilies can also be grown from seed which takes even longer. Sow the seed in deep boxes or half pots in a well-drained compost. A proprietary seed compost with extra coarse sand or grit will do. Sow the seed in autumn as soon as it is ripe and maintain a temperature of 16°C (61°F) and good light. If these conditions are difficult to provide, it is preferable to sow the seed in spring

species and varieties	Not all lilies thrive in pots. Some of those that do are *L.* 'Connecticut King' and *L.* 'Black Dragon' (easy lilies for beginners, being vigorous and lime-tolerant), the cultivars and varieties of *L. speciosum* (which need ericaceous compost), *L. auratum* and *L. formosanum*, the latter being easily grown from seed. (See also p.99)

 HOT WATER PLANT
(Achimenes 'Little Beauty'*)*

These small, showy plants were great favourites of the Victorians and it was believed that they needed to be watered with hot water to start them into growth. Moist compost at the proper temperature, however, does just as well. They are perfect plants for the window-sills of shady conservatories and are very easy to grow and to increase.

category	Cool and shady
type	Deciduous perennial
flowers	Trumpet-shaped, crimson-pink
leaves	Oval, toothed, dark green
height	25cm (10in)
spread	30cm (12in)
temperature	16°C (61°F) to start tiny tubers into growth
position	Good light but no direct sun
planting	Pot up the small tubers, six to a 13cm (5in) pot, about 2.5cm (1in) deep, at any time from late winter to mid-spring if the right heat can be maintained. Water sparingly with warm water
compost	JI No. 2 or a peat-based, all-purpose compost
care	Do not overwater the new growth which should be visible three weeks after planting. Pinch out the tips at third pairs of leaves to increase bushiness. Feed in the autumn
propagation	The planted tubers will have produced up to six new tubers each. These can remain in the pots provided they are kept dry and frost free. The following spring, select the largest of the tubers and pot them up as before
species and varieties	*A.* 'Peach Blossom' is trailing and peach coloured; *A.* 'Topsy' is pale blue and *A.* 'Camberwell Beauty' is pink

practical
project
1

QUICK COLOUR
FOR THE
CONSERVATORY

**ANNUAL CLIMBERS OR
CLIMBERS THAT CAN BE
GROWN AS ANNUALS**

Cobaea scandens (Cup and saucer
vine)
Eccremocarpus scaber (Chilean
glory flower)
Ipomoea lobata (syn. *Mina lobata*)
I. tricolor (Morning glory)
Nasturtiums
Rhodochiton atrosanguineus
Thunbergia alata (Black-eyed
Susan)

An empty conservatory can be quite daunting, especially if you've only just acquired it. You do not know how hot it will get or how low the temperature will fall in the winter. You may never have grown tender plants before or had experience of growing under glass. However, there are sensible steps that can be taken. If you and your conservatory first meet in winter, then the best thing to do is to put in a maximum and minimum thermometer and keep a note of the lowest temperatures through the season. In the summer, while you should also keep a note of temperatures and make observations on how easy it is to ventilate, you do not need to look at an empty space.

In a sunny conservatory, you will be safe to put in pelargoniums, cacti and succulent plants, which survive even if the temperature rockets, but unless you have a very large number of these, the conservatory will still seem empty. Expensive 'conservatory' plants ordered through the post can be very small, so are not always the best bet. What can you do?

VEGETABLES AND FRUIT

Grow annual and fast growing perennial climbers! They do not have to be ornamental plants. Tender runner and climbing pole beans take on a luxuriant appearance when grown under cover, and can be obtained with scarlet, scarlet and white, pink, white and purple flowers. For yellow flowers, grow cucumbers and melons; they will quickly cover a wall. Other decorative vegetables are aubergines and sweet peppers, again available in different colours and sizes.

All these are gross feeders and need large containers. Grow bags are inexpensive but are not very attractive. They are, however, the cheapest way of buying the amount of compost you need which can then be transferred to other containers. Old buckets with holes in, painted cans, and willow and wicker baskets lined with plastic carrier bags or bin liners, are all less conspicuous. Old or new chimney pots have a good depth for root growth. Large terracotta and ceramic pots are wonderful. Try lining unglazed pots with polythene to prevent too much water loss throught the sides.

GROWING FROM SEED

Seed can be sown this month as follows:
■ Sow seeds of melons in seed trays at a temperature of 18°C (64°F). Transfer the seedlings to growing bags or 23–25cm (9–10in) pots and support the plants on wires or canes as they grow. For serious fruit production, pinch out the growing point when the main shoot is 2m (6½ft) long to encourage side shoots.

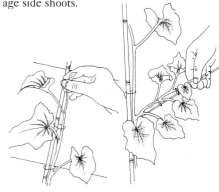

■ Cucumbers need a temperature of 20°C (68°F) for germination. They do not transplant well, so sow the seeds directly into larger pots or grow bags or use peat pots. Pinch the tops out after five or six leaves have appeared.

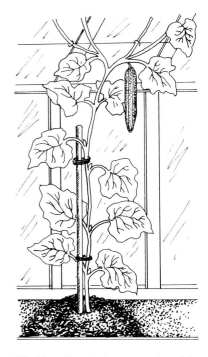

■ Climbing French beans need a rich soil and a temperature of 12°C (54°F) to germinate. Sow five beans to a 20cm (8in) pot of good compost and keep well-watered. They will wind themselves round strings, canes or large mesh nylon netting fixed to the wall.

ORNAMENTALS

Flowering annuals, or perennials that flower in their first year from seed provide cheap and cheerful colour for the conservatory over a long period. These range from the well known Morning glory, *Ipomoea tricolor* 'Heavenly Blue', and Black-eyed Susan, *Thunbergia alata*, to plants that are usually grown out of doors, like *Cobaea scandens* and nasturtiums. Seeds for all these are widely available.

There are also several useful annuals that are less often seen. You may need to approach a specialist seed supplier (often listed in the back of gardening magazines) for seeds of *Lophospermum erubescens* and the closely related *Maurandya barclaiana* and *M. scandens*. These all used to be known as Asarinas and can still be found in catalogues under that name. They have tubular flowers, like foxgloves, in shades of pink, mauve and purple, and hoist themselves up by means of thier leaf stalks, in the same way that a clematis does. *Rhodochiton atrosanguineus* climbs in the same way and has striking tubular, deep purple flowers which hang from pagoda-like calyces. It is long flowering. *Lablab purpureus*, the Australian pea, also known as *Dolichos lablab*, has purply pink or white pea flowers which give way to long seed pods with edible seeds.

The Morning glory has fast-growing relations, such as *Ipomoea quamoclit* and *I. lobata*. You will find these in seed catalogues under a variety of names including convolvulus, quamoclit, ipomea or mina: they are all the same family. Look for the annual climbing varieties. The lovely trumpet flowers of the ipomoeas are available in sky-blue, purple and magenta. *I. coccinea* (syn. *Q. coccinea*) has scarlet flowers with a yellow throat, while *Mina lobata* (syn. *Q. lobata*) has delicate narrow flowers that change from red, through orange and yellow to white.

USING BABY PLANTS

Another way of adding inexpensive foliage plants to a new conservatory is to buy fast-growing baby plants that are sold in garden shops and centres for planting 'in hanging baskets. Trailers to look out for are *Plectranthus australis*, the incense-scented Swedish ivy, and Ground ivy (*Glechoma hederacea* 'Variegata').

plants
OF THE
month
2

BLACK-EYED SUSAN
(Thunbergia alata)

T. alata flowers prolifically until well into autumn. From a packet of seeds you can get flowers of all shades from orange to yellow and white. Several plants in a pot, grown up a wigwam of canes, make a very pretty feature with all the varied yet harmonizing colours.

category	Easy
type	Annual climber
flowers	Rounded flat, orange to white, with dark brown centres; summer into autumn
leaves	Pointed, heart-shaped
height	1.8m (6ft)
spread	30cm (1ft)
temperature	4°C (40°F)
position	Good light
planting	Transfer seedlings three to a 15cm (6in) pot. Train plants up slender canes
compost	JI No. 2
care	Water freely during the growing season and give regular liquid feeds
propagation	Sow seeds from early spring at a temperature of 18–24°C (65–75°F)
species and varieties	*T. grandiflora* is a vigorous evergreen species with pale blue flowers. *T. mysorensis* has 45cm (18in) racemes of yellow flowers marked with brownish red. *T. gregorii* has glowing orange flowers. These are all perennials

CUP AND SAUCER VINE
(Cobaea scandens)

The 'Cup and saucer' vine is usually grown out of doors, but in a large pot or a conservatory border it can put on a phenomenal amount of growth and cover a large wall in one season. Indeed, it could be persuaded to cover the roof to shade the conservatory. It is free flowering and has a graceful habit.

category	Easy
type	Perennial climber
flowers	Open yellow-green and age to violet-purple, fragrant. Each sits on a pale green calyx, resembling the cup and saucer of its common name; summer to autumn
leaves	4–6 oval leaflets
height	4–5m (12–15ft)
spread	4–5m (12–15ft)
temperature	3–7°C (38–45°F) if you want to treat it as a perennial
position	Full sun
planting	Transplant to as large a pot as possible, minimum 22cm (9in), or a trough or border in early summer
compost	Any good multipurpose compost
care	Water freely during growing season. Provide weak high potash feed from late summer. Prune back long shoots in autumn to overwinter the plant
propagation	Sow seed in early spring at a temperature of 16–18°C (60–65°F)
species and varieties	*C. scandens alba* has whitish flowers

practical project 2

MAKING SIMPLE ROOF BLINDS

INSTANT BLINDS
For those not handy with a sewing machine, green plastic mesh can be used. This does not need hemming and can be fixed in the same way, with the hems to hold the canes at each end, stapled in place. Treat lengths of dowelling with a green stain to give an attractive finish.

If you can machine a straight seam you can make these simple blinds for the inside of the conservatory roof. Beige curtain lining is the cheapest fabric to use. It diffuses the sunlight, reduces glare and can be left in place all summer. If you use a darker fabric that gives more shade, you would need to be able to take it down easily on dull days.

YOU WILL NEED

Sewing machine
Tape measure
Scissors, Pins
Fabric, 1m (1yd) wide and sufficiently long to cover the area of your conservatory roof
Sewing cotton
Bamboo canes or lengths of dowelling, not more than 12.5mm ($^1/_2$in) diameter
Note *It is preferable to buy short canes and cut them into sections rather than long ones. Short canes are thinner and it is easier to rest two overlapping canes in each cup-hook*
Cup-hooks (for a wooden conservatory), or cropped-headed nuts and bolts which slot and twist into glazing bars (for an aluminium-framed building)
Plastic channelling for electric cables

■ Measure the roof and decide how many widths of fabric will be needed and what length they should be.

■ Add 15cm (6in) extra on to each length and 4cm (1$^1/_2$in) on to the width to allow for hems. The blinds look best if they are the same width as the space between the glazing bars or, if these are too narrow, covering two widths of glass.

■ Hem the sides of the fabric first.

■ Then make two open-ended hems 2.5cm (1in) deep at the top and bottom of each length. This is to hold a bamboo pole or length of narrow dowelling which should be longer than the fabric is wide.

■ For a wooden-framed conservatory, screw the cup-hooks into the highest wooden cross beam, either the conservatory ridge or the beam fixed to the house wall.

■ Screw the remaining cup-hooks to the beam at the eaves of the conservatory roof.

■ Slide the bamboo poles into the hems of the blinds and support the canes in the cup-hooks. The fabric will sag and needs to be supported at least once. It may be possible to loop it through gaps between cross beams and the glass but if there are no suitable beams, screw additional cup-hooks into glazing bars and support the material with more bamboo canes or lengths of dowelling.

ALUMINIUM CONSERVATORIES

■ With an aluminium-framed conservatory or lean-to greenhouse, it will be necessary to drill into the house wall to insert the hooks.

■ To fix the blinds at the outer frame, it is simple, if fiddly, to attach a length of plastic cable channelling or other inconspicuous bar, using cropped-headed bolts and nuts.

■ You will need to drill holes in the back half of the plastic channelling to line up with the glazing bars.

■ Push the bolts into the holes from the back.

■ Then slot the heads into the groove on the glazing bars. Do this one at a time, screwing each nut on and ensuring that the rectangular heads are locked in at right angles to the groove.

■ Once the channelling is in place, clip the front section on. The blind can be tucked behind it. Put the cane in afterwards.

■ Alternatively, small curtain weights can be sewn into the end or you can add a fringe or other decorative edging to add to the 'tented' appearance.

■ For the rooflight, it is simpler to use a fixed piece of fabric over the light and use separate pieces before and beyond it.

CLEANING

Blinds made from beige curtain lining can be given a cool wash (40°C). Coloured fabric will need testing first. Plastic mesh can be soaked in a solution of floor and wall cleaning powder.

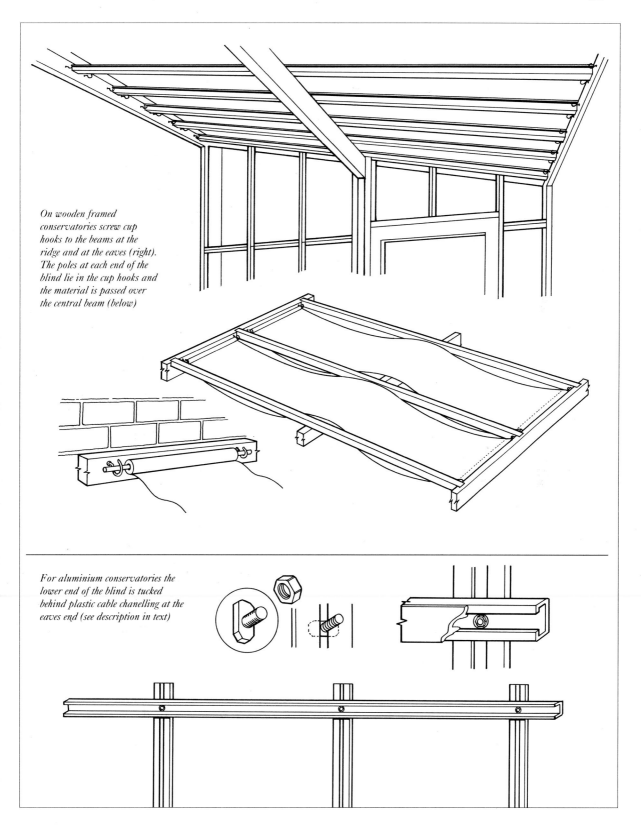

On wooden framed conservatories screw cup hooks to the beams at the ridge and at the eaves (right). The poles at each end of the blind lie in the cup hooks and the material is passed over the central beam (below)

For aluminium conservatories the lower end of the blind is tucked behind plastic cable chanelling at the eaves end (see description in text)

J U N E

Early summer can be overwhelming in its abundance: the conservatory gardener is torn between the plants in the conservatory and those in the garden, all of them, seemingly, flowering with abandon. Fuchsias, begonias, sinningias, pelargoniums, heliotropes and streptocarpus are in bloom this month. Exotic climbers like the bougainvilleas, passion flowers and stephanotis will also be demanding attention.

In the middle of a sunny day a conservatory facing full sun will be too hot to linger in unless it is extremely well-ventilated and shaded. This is the time to consider putting as many of these plants as possible outside – they will enjoy the air and lower temperature as much as you do. Leave the conservatory to the plants that like it. Olives, oleanders, zonal pelargoniums, and cacti and succulents can all take any amount of heat and bright sunlight. In a conservatory which regularly registers over 32°C (90°F) anything else that is movable can be put outside with advantage.

A large proportion of conservatory activity during the summer will be in connection with watering, shading, ventilating and pest control. But, however difficult, try to make time for some of the tasks that will make next winter and early spring more like summer in the conservatory. Seeds can be sown and cuttings taken which will need no additional heat. Primulas, cinerarias and succulents can all be propagated. There should be sufficient colour in the conservatory but look around to see if the display would benefit from more rich, green foliage plants. Those with large leaves add a tropical rainforest effect that fits well with the summer temperature. You need to be able to provide the humidity they need, though. Leafy climbers make a splendid green canopy at this time of year. The leaves of Campsis radicans *for example seem unfazed by the sun and because it is deciduous, this climber which can stand a certain amount of frost does not shade the conservatory during the winter or spring. Grape vines have the same advantages.*

tasks

FOR THE

month

ROUTINE TASKS

Leave windows, rooflights and louvres open at night if temperature is 16°C (61°F) or above. Shade the conservatory during the day

Examine pots daily to check water requirements. Plants that are in bloom or are making growth should be watered well each day. Spray palms, ferns and foliage plants with soft water daily

Feed growing plants regularly

Rooted cuttings of pelargonium, fuchsia and carnation should be in final pots for autumn display

Regal pelargoniums that have finished flowering can be cut back

Move pot-grown roses, jasmine and solanum outside

Sow seeds of cineraria, *Primula malacoides*, *P. kewensis* and calceolarias for autumn and winter-flowering displays

Stake any lilies that are growing very tall. Support other plants as necessary, with light twigs

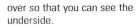

CHECKLIST

☐ Increase humidity
☐ Take cuttings
☐ Root strawberry runners

INCREASING HUMIDITY

Keeping the right amount of moisture in the atmosphere so that plants thrive, yet people are not uncomfortable, is difficult. This is where the solid-floored conservatory comes into its own as it can easily be damped down on a hot day simply by throwing a jug of water over the floor. The shelves and benches can be sprayed, using a hosepipe to save time. For the best effect this should be done in the middle of the day.

Conservatories or garden rooms with cushions, carpets and other soft furnishings must be treated in a different way.

■ Group plants together, so they create their own humidity.

■ Put plants on plastic trays of gravel or other proprietary aggregate and keep it damp. The pots should not be sitting in water but above it.

■ Many plants can be given a humid microclimate by placing them in their pot inside a larger pot, and filling the space between with moist

peat or sand. Keep the peat or sand permanently moist.

■ Mist the plants regularly with a fine spray.

■ Some plants may need watering twice a day, in the morning and late afternoon.

■ Install a capillary watering system. (See p.77.)

TAKING LEAF CUTTINGS

If you want to increase your stock of some of the most showy conservatory plants, now is the time to try. Midsummer is the season to take leaf cuttings of streptocarpus, *Begonia rex*, African violets and gloxinia (sinningia).

Begonias
■ Fill a half-size seed tray with a mixture of sand and peat or a proprietary cuttings compost.

■ Take a healthy young leaf and stalk from the plant and insert the stalk into the compost so that the back surface of the leaf lies flat on the compost. Roots will develop from the leaf axil.

■ If you want to make more plants from one leaf, turn it

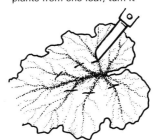

over so that you can see the underside.

■ Make a small incision about 1.25cm (¹/₂in) long across the biggest veins with a sharp knife.

■ Then place the leaf, underside down, onto the compost. The cut surfaces need to be in contact with the compost so you may need to pin or weigh the leaf down.

■ The leaf cuttings need a warm, humid atmosphere, so put the seed tray in a propagator at a temperature of 16–18°C (61–64°F) or cover it with a polythene bag and place it in a warm corner of the conservatory but out of direct sunlight.

■ When the plantlets have formed, detach them carefully from the leaf and pot them up.

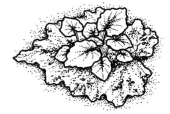

Streptocarpus

For streptocarpus follow the same basic method. Small streptocarpus leaves can be used whole, or large leaves can be cut into sections. (See Plants of the Month p.79.)

Taking leaf cuttings

Saintpaulias (African violets) and sinningia

These can also be increased by leaf cuttings.

■ Take leaves with about 5cm (2in) of stalk and insert them singly into 6cm (2½in) pots; keep them at a temperature of 18–21°C (64–70°). Pot on as necessary.

Tip cuttings

Philodendrons can be propagated by tip cuttings.

■ Take 10–15cm (4–6in) long tip cuttings that include a mature leaf.

■ Insert them individually in 8–10cm (3–4in) pots containing peat and keep in a warm, humid atmosphere at 21–24°C (70–75°F). Pieces of stem with one or two joints will also root under these conditions.

■ To propagate ivies (*Hedera* species and cultivars), take 8–13cm (3–5in) tip cuttings at any time during the summer.

■ To make an ivy bush, take the cuttings from adult growth, the flowering and fruiting shoots.

Taking tip cuttings

■ To produce climbing plants, take the cuttings from runner growth which has lobed leaves and aerial roots.

■ Root all cuttings in equal parts of peat and sand and in a polythene covered pot. They will not need any extra heat.

ROUTINE TASKS

Thin grapes: a three year old vine should have three bunches only, and a four year old, five bunches. The bunches themselves will also need thinning to allow the individual grapes room to swell

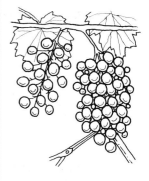

Check hydrangea plants to see if there are shoots that can be used for cuttings

Red spider mite and other pests can be a problem so check your plants regularly. (See p.47 for control measures)

ROOTING STRAWBERRY RUNNERS

If you plan to grow strawberries in pots in the conservatory for early crops next year, now is a good time to begin the process. As soon as strawberries have finished fruiting out-of-doors, they begin to put out runners. Space the runners out evenly round the plant so that each plantlet which develops has room to grow. The small plants can be potted up after one to two months for forcing the following year.

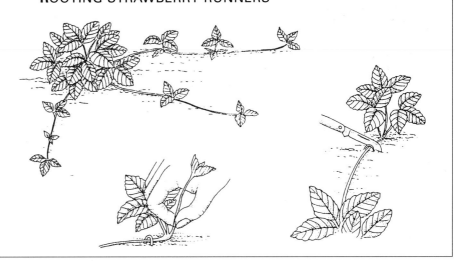

plants
OF THE
month

HYDRANGEA
(*Hydrangea arborescens* 'Annabelle')

The huge flower heads of *H. arborescens* 'Annabelle' surpass even those of the ordinary hydrangea. Although it is quite hardy and can be grown in the garden, the protection of the conservatory ensures perfect undamaged flowers, much earlier. They create an opulent Victorian effect in the conservatory during a period when the garden outdoors is exerting powerful competition.

category	Easy
type	Hardy, deciduous shrub
flowers	Huge rounded heads of white, four-petalled 'flowers' (actually showy sepals) 20cm (8in) and more across
leaves	Broad, pointed, oval, bright green
height	1.2–1.8m (4–6ft)
spread	1.2m (4ft)
temperature	Unheated
position	Partial shade
planting	23cm (9in) pots
compost	JI No. 2 or 3
care	Hydrangeas must be kept well-watered at all times, but particularly while they are in flower. After flowering, cut stems back to two pairs of leaves and repot (or plant outdoors)
propagation	Take 10–15cm (4–6in) cuttings from non-flowering shoots in late

Fuchsia 'Thalia'

summer or early autumn. Use equal parts peat and sand and give bottom heat of 13–16ºC (55–61ºF). After rooting, pot on successively up to a 23cm (9in) pot. Pinch out growing points after three pairs of leaves have formed, to promote compact and bushy growth

species and varieties	All *H. macrophylla* varieties and cultivars, hortensias and lacecaps will do well under glass and need the same treatment. Many unnamed cultivars can be bought as pot plants – an easy and inexpensive way of acquiring hydrangeas if you cannot beg cuttings from friends. For blue flowers from cultivars like *H.* 'Blue Wave', *H.* 'Générale Vicomtesse de Vibraye' or *H.* 'Hamburg', use a lime-free compost and water with rainwater

STEPHANOTIS
(*Stephanotis floribunda*)

Frequently grown as a pot plant, its long stems wreathed round a wire frame, stephanotis is known for its marvellous scent. The pure white flowers contrast sharply with the dark gleaming leaves and last for a long period over the summer.

category	Challenging
type	Evergreen, twining climber
flowers	Waxy, white, trumpet-like, in clusters
leaves	Glossy, thick, oval, about 7cm (3in) long
height	5m (15ft) and more
temperature	Will survive temperatures of 10ºC (50ºF) but will do better at 13ºC (55ºF). Sudden falls in temperature may be responsible for plant's well-known refusal to flower
position	Light shade in summer but full light at other times is essential for flowering
planting	12–15cm (5–6in) pots or in conservatory border. Train shoots up wires and strings and along roof if in border, or round canes if in pots
compost	JI No. 2 with some extra sand
care	Keep plants just moist in winter; humid and warm in summer. Pot on each year in mid-spring until plants are in 23cm (9in) pots. Then repot only every three years. Fortnightly

high-potash liquid feed from late spring to early autumn. Can be pruned back by reducing lateral growths to 7cm (3in) and main shoots to half

propagation Take 10cm (4in) semi-ripe cuttings and root in equal parts sand and peat at 20ºC (68ºF) in early summer

FUCHSIA
(*Fuchsia* 'Thalia')

The pendent flowers of the fuchsia are made up of petals, a tube and sepals, often in two different shades. Free-flowering over a long period, they are very popular in tubs, baskets and the border, as well as under glass. *F.* 'Thalia' has particularly good leaves which form an excellent background for the vivid orange-red flowers. It needs a slightly higher temperature than many other hybrids. In general, the smaller-flowered hybrids like *F.* 'Alice Hoffman', with carmine sepals and double, white petals, are frost-hardy, while those with larger flowers, such as *F.* 'Swingtime', which has bright red sepals and white petals, are more tender.

category Cool and shady
type Small, deciduous shrub
flowers Orange-red, tubular, in hanging terminal clusters
leaves Dark green with a silk sheen, reddish beneath
height 40–90cm (15–36in)
spread 30–60cm (12–24in)
temperature Minimum 4ºC (39ºF)
position Good light but not direct sun
planting 15–23cm (6–9in) pots
compost JI No. 3
care In an unheated conservatory, cut plants back hard and keep on the dry side in a shady place. If large plants are wanted then maintain a temperature of 13ºC (55ºF) and pot on each spring until in a 23cm (9in) pot. Keep pinching back shoots every second leaf for a bushy plant. In early spring trim plants lightly, water and start into growth at 10ºC (50ºF). Feed with high-nitrogen fertilizer, followed by a high potash liquid manure like Tomorite when in flower
propagation 8–10cm (3–4in) tip cuttings in early spring. Root individually in 5cm (2in) pots of cuttings compost mixed with equal volume of sand. Keep at 16ºC (61ºF)

species and *F.* 'Cascade', has red-tinged, white
varieties sepals, deep pink petals and a drooping habit which makes it ideal for hanging baskets. *F.* 'Ting-a-ling' is very free-flowering with white flowers. Fuchsia species need more heat. *F. procumbens* is a prostrate shrub with small yellow flowers, purple sepals and bright blue pollen

HELIOTROPE

(*Heliotropium arborescens*)

The common name of the heliotrope, cherry pie, is very apt as it really does smell deliciously like one. The tiny flowers, in corymbs 5–7cm (2–3in) across, vary in colour from almost white to deep violet. They have a long flowering season.

category Fragrant
type Small, evergreen sub-shrub
flowers Small forget-me-not flowers in clusters, from pale mauve to violet
leaves Mid-green, textured, finely creased
height 30–45cm (12–18in) as a pot plant
spread 30–40cm (12–15in)
temperature 4ºC (39ºF), cool
position As much light as possible, slightly shaded in summer. Good ventilation
planting 10–15cm (4–6in) pots. It flowers best when pot-bound
compost JI No. 2
care Water generously during summer. Keep just moist in winter. Repot in early spring if necessary. Be sparing with fertilizer; a weak feed once every three weeks is enough. Prune regularly to keep in shape
propagation Take 8–10cm (3–4in) cuttings in early autumn or late winter. Root in a mixture of equal parts peat and sand at 16–18ºC (61–64ºF). Pot on into 8cm (3in) pots of JI No. 1. Seed may be sown in seed compost at the same temperature. Pinch out when 8cm (3in) high to encourage bushy growth
species and *H.* 'Lord Roberts' and *H.* 'Princess
varieties Marina' are guaranteed fragrant; it is worth seeking out one of the specialist nurseries that still sell them. Seeds are more widely available. Avoid *H.* 'Marine' which, although described as fragrant, is disappointing. Try the variety listed in catalogues as *H.* x *hybridum peruvianum.* Paler flowers are reputed to have the best perfume

practical project

TRAINING A STANDARD PLANT

Forming a bushy head on a standard coleus

The term 'standard' when applied to trees refers to a tree with a 1.8m (6ft) clear stem. In the conservatory, however, the term is used for an ornamental plant on a clear stem of *any* height. Standard fuchsias are well-known occupants of greenhouses and conservatories that do not get full sun. The pendent flowers and arching stems of many cultivars make them ideal subjects for training.

In the garden, roses are frequently trained as standards and occasionally so is wisteria. However, other plants can be trained to produce a round head of flowers and leaves on top of a clear stem. Many tender plants look very effective trained this way and can be a dramatic focal point in the conservatory.

Many of the plants suggested here can be bought in spring as 'baby' plants or rooted cuttings in garden centres, particularly fuchsias, pelargoniums, *Chrysanthemum frutescens*, *Euryops pectinatus* and *Lantana camara*. There should be a good range of different varieties and colours to choose from.

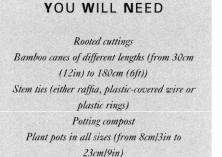

YOU WILL NEED

Rooted cuttings
Bamboo canes of different lengths (from 30cm (12in) to 180cm (6ft))
Stem ties (either raffia, plastic-covered wire or plastic rings)

Potting compost
Plant pots in all sizes (from 8cm/3in to 23cm/9in)

Coleus
Particularly exciting and good for all-year colour is a standard solenostemon, better known as coleus, the flame nettle. They are very fast-growing and cuttings will root easily at any time of the year. Coleus are very variable in leaf pattern, even on the same plant, and any non-flowering shoot that is particularly distinctive or attractive can be used for cuttings.

■ Select short-jointed shoots 5–8cm (2–3in) long, remove the lowest pair of leaves and trim below a node.

■ Insert the cuttings in seed and cuttings compost and put the pot in a propagator or a plastic bag at a temperature of 21°C (70°F). Cuttings can also be rooted in jars of water.

■ When rooted, pot the plants into 9cm (3½in) pots of JI No. 2 soil-based compost.

■ Tie the leading shoot to a short cane until it has reached the desired size – probably between 60–90cm (2–3ft) – then pinch out the tip.

■ The side shoots at the top will grow out and the tips of these should be pinched out when the shoots are 5cm (2in) long.

■ Coleus need to be kept at an even 16°C (61°F) during the winter and should be brought into the house if the conservatory is not maintained at that temperature.

Pelargonium

For a small standard, the pelargonium, *P. crispum* 'Variegatum', is very effective. The best time to take cuttings is in mid- to late summer, but they will root at almost any time. Proceed as for the coleus, but while the leading shoot is growing to the required height, do not remove all the leaves from the stem. Pinch out the tips of the side shoots but allow one or two leaves to remain in place. These feed the stem and help it to become strong. The pinched-out shoots will root in their turn, producing yet more plants if desired. Pelargoniums are frost tender, that is, hardy to 1°C (34°F), and can remain in a frost-free conservatory all year.

Fuchsia

To train standard fuchsias, first select cuttings from vigorous, upright species. *F.* 'Tennessee Waltz', *F.* 'White Ann' and *F.* 'Hidcote Beauty' are suitable. *F.* 'Lady Thumb' makes a delightful miniature standard.

■ Fuchsia cuttings can be taken at any time of the year, root very easily and can be either tip cuttings, sections of stem or single leaf cuttings.

■ Cut below a node with the tip and three sets of leaves.

■ Remove the two lower sets before inserting the cuttings into a compost of half peat and half sharp sand or a product like Perlite or Vermiculite.

■ Once the rooted cutting has begun to grow, transplant it to a 6cm (2¹/₂in) pot of potting compost. Fuchsias must be potted on regularly to prevent the stem growing too woody and causing premature flowering. The largest size pot should be 23cm (9in).

■ As the leader grows, it must be supported by a cane to ensure the stem grows straight. Tie the stem to the cane every 5cm (2in) if necessary.

■ When the leader has reached the height you want, let three sets of leaves develop, then pinch out the growing tip.

■ Leave any leaves on the stem until the head has been formed.

■ Every time the side shoots have made two or three pairs of leaves, pinch out the growing tip. Do this until the diameter of the head is in a good proportion to the length of the stem. Flowers should appear from six to ten weeks after the final pinching out.

A standard fuchsia should not be kept in a sunny conservatory at the height of summer; stand them outside in a partly-shaded position and bring them indoors as the weather cools.

Standards from the other plants listed are formed in the same way. Some will need staking throughout their lives, like the solenostemon (coleus) and the Paris daisy, *Chrysanthemum frutescens*, which can develop very large heads. Others, which form sturdier trunks, can have the stake removed, eventually. Woody-stemmed plants, like bay or cassia, take several years to grow to the desired height but the principles are the same. Stems of brugmansias should be allowed to grow to about 1.2m (4ft) before the tops are pinched out. Prune to shape every year in late winter.

PLANTS SUITABLE FOR TRAINING AS STANDARDS

Anisodontea capensis
Brugmansias
Cassia corymbosa
'Charm' chrysanthemums
Chrysanthemum frutescens or
   Paris daisy
Coleus (*Solenostemon*)
Euryops pectinatus
Fuchsias, some cvs.
Heliotropium arborescens
Lantana camara
Laurus nobilis or **bay tree**
Myrtus communis ssp. **tarentina**
Pelargoniums, some cvs.
Polygala myrtifolia and
   P. × *dalmaisiana*

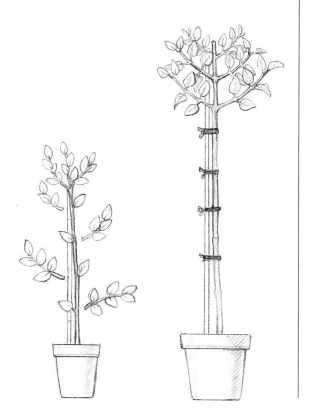

JULY

Some of the most eye-catching conservatory plants are in flower now. The spectacular trumpets of the brugmansias (daturas), the satiny glow of hibiscus flowers and the dense efflorescence of oleanders vie for attention. In a shady conservatory, fuchsias and streptocarpus will be at their best.

Keeping a high level of humidity during hot weather is important now. Red spider mites love a hot dry situation and brugmansias. An infestation quickly turns the large, soft leaves from a rich green to a pallid and mottled one, much reducing the vigour of the plant.

Other plants that suffer from drought are Polygala myrtifolia, Hydrangea arborescens, prostantheras and leptospermums. After a long dry period, many shrubs and herbaceous plants will come back and surprise you, but not these. When you go on holiday, try to make special, foolproof arrangements for their care.

For the usual two-week summer holiday, place plants in a deep tray of water on the table by the window of a deeply shaded room in the house. This will keep most of them alive. Even in summer the temperature should be cool enough to prevent too much lank growth but not too cool to encourage moulds and rot. The bath is another useful place for temporarily keeping plants in pots.

In a crowded conservatory, you can be sure that it is the pots containing the most drought-sensitive plants that will somehow be overlooked. One answer to this perennial summer problem is to grow succulent plants or cacti – plants designed to cope with long periods without water. There is an amazing variety of leaf colour, form and habit in these plants. The 'elephant bush' or 'money plant', Portulacaria afra, will fill a pot 46cm (18in) across in time and make a magnificent specimen. Neglect and a summer baking help to ensure it flowers. Another succulent plant that becomes more magnificent as it matures is the purple-leaved Aeonium arboreum atropurpureum.

tasks
FOR THE
month

CAMELLIAS AND AZALEAS
After camellias and azaleas have finished flowering, they begin to put on growth. By midsummer they stop growing and start to form flower buds for the next year. They should be stood outside in a shady spot and it is important that they are well-watered during this period.

CHECKLIST

☐ Sow seeds
☐ Make holiday watering arrangements

SOWING SEEDS

The high temperature in the conservatory can be used for germinating the seeds of many tender species this month, such as palms, citrus fruits, strelitzia, lobelia, cineraria and schizanthus.

Avocados and citrus fruits
These plants have seeds that produce interesting conservatory plants.

■ Soak avocado stones in lukewarm water in a warm place for two days and then plant in a sandy compost, in 10cm (4in) pots in a temperature of 21°C (70°F), ensuring that the more pointed end of the stone is at the top.

■ Another method is to soak the stone in hot water (50°C/ 122°F) and then cut 1.25cm (¹/₂in) off the pointed end.

■ Dip the cut end in a fungicide and plant as before.

■ Alternatively, suspend the stone in a jar of warm water, with the round end (from which the root will emerge) in the water. The jar will need to be kept warm and topped up regularly.

■ As soon as the shoot is 15cm (6in) tall, cut off the top 8cm (3in) and the plant will put out a side shoot.

■ Pinch out the growing tip of this and further shoots when they are 15cm (6in) long, to encourage a bushy habit.

■ Pips from citrus fruits are unlikely to breed true if they are germinated in the ordinary way, but they will still produce attractive plants with fragrant flowers. A temperature of 16–21°C (61–70°F) is necessary. Sow the pips individually and cover with a plastic lid or polythene bag. A small modular seed tray is ideal for this.

Palms
Soak the seeds overnight and then sow in moist peat at 21–24°C (70–75°F). *Chamaerops humilis* should germinate in about a fortnight; other palms may take up to six months. *Phoenix canariensis* and *Trachycarpus fortunei* should be sown in a temperature of 24°C (75°F).

■ Now that fresh dates are available all year round, it is fun to try to germinate the seeds of the date palm, *Phoenix dactylifera.*

■ Collect as many seeds as you can and soak them in lukewarm water for two days.

■ Then sow them in moist seed compost, covering them well with the compost.

■ Keep them tightly covered, in a warm place and watch for germination. The root will appear first and the seed can then be potted up in an 8cm (3in) pot filled with peat or peat alternative-based compost.

■ Repot as necessary but do not over-pot.

Strelitzia
■ Strelitzia seed must be soaked for 24 hours.

■ The seed can then be sown in moist sand in a polythene bag. This should be kept in the dark at a temperature of 21–24°C (70–75°F) (the airing cupboard is ideal).

■ Examine the bag regularly, removing and potting up any seeds that have germinated. (For further information about strelitzias, see p.36.)

Banana
The procedure for germinating banana seed (*Musa* species including *M. ensete* and *M. basjoo*) is similar to strelitzias but they need a higher temperature of 27°C (80°F) for between one and six months.

Cineraria, lobelia and schizanthus
The seeds of cinerarias, lobelias and schizanthus are sown in the usual way (see p.23). Cinerarias sown now will flower in winter. After germination the seedlings should be moved to the cold frame after they have been potted up. Six lobelia seedlings can be pricked out into a 13cm (5in) pot to flower from midsummer to early autumn next year. Schizanthus sown now will germinate in a few days and should be pricked out immediately. Re-pot soon after and every time they need it. By next spring they should be flowering in 19cm (7¹/₂in) pots.

GOING ON HOLIDAY

Even if all pots have been put outside, you cannot rely on rain to water them this month. Make sure that special plants have been put in a shady place and, if possible, plunge the pots in ashes, gravel or damp peat to keep them moist. Water the plunge beds well before you leave and clay pots too as they can often absorb sufficient moisture to keep their occupants alive. There are several species that must *not* be allowed to dry out, either at this time of year or any time. Azaleas and camellias will be making their flower buds for next year at this time and should be kept well-watered with soft water. It may be worth asking a neighbour to look after them.

Hydrangeas, leptospermums and polygalas need to have their roots moist at all times, particularly during the growing season, and are unlikely to recover from a drying out.

■ A planting trough of 46cm (18in) deep and 46cm (18in) wide should remain moist for two weeks if you give it a good soaking then thickly mulch the top with gravel or black polythene sheet before you go away.

■ Several large pots will fit into the bath (line the bottom with towels) or on gravel trays in the windows of shady rooms for a week or two but these are very temporary measures and if long absences are planned, it is probably worth investing in a more permanent watering system.

■ There are numerous watering systems on the market that allow a small amount of water to be dripped through pipes, either permanently or with the aid of a computerized timer. These can be the answer for plants that are permanently planted in a border. The systems vary in complexity, from simple drip or capillary systems that run off a tap to properly plumbed-in seep hoses for the borders. There is even a new pumped system that works with stored rainwater from a butt or tank: well worth considering if you are in a hard-water area and grow many lime-hating plants in the conservatory. (See Useful Addresses p.138.)

The capillary method of watering is illustrated below.

(See Useful Addresses p.138.)

ROUTINE TASKS

ROUTINE TASKS

Rooflights and ventilators can be left open all the time

Continue to water plants at least once and probably two or three times daily and to damp down the floor and shelves if possible

Begonias, gloxinias, fuchsias, campanulas, heliotropes and zonal pelargoniums should be in full flower. Shade the plants during sunny weather and give ample ventilation, from early in the morning. Temperatures can rise excessively as the day progresses. Shade and coolness encourage long blooming

Plant autumn-flowering bulbs like *Amaryllis belladonna* and nerines

Take cuttings of regal pelargoniums and hydrangeas

Remove any debris such as old compost or defunct annual plants to the compost heap

Move out spring-flowering pot plants to a shaded cold frame

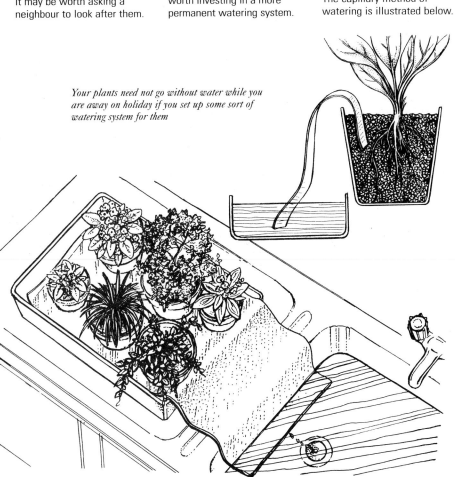

Your plants need not go without water while you are away on holiday if you set up some sort of watering system for them

WATERING LIME-HATERS

Azaleas, camellias and heathers are well-known lime-haters. Correas, citrus, many epiphytes and some lilies also dislike alkaline conditions. This needs to be taken into account when watering, particularly if you live in a hard-water area.

plants

OF THE

month

1

 TRUMPET VINE
(Campsis radicans)

In a long hot summer this self-clinging, almost hardy climber will flower out-of-doors late in the season. Under glass it will flower from midsummer to mid-autumn every year and provide a dappled green canopy from late spring.

category	Easy
type	Deciduous climber
flowers	6cm (2½in) long coral-red trumpets in clusters
leaves	Made up of 7–11 oval leaflets with toothed edges
height	4.5–9m (15–30ft)
temperature	0°C (32°F)
position	Sunny
planting	In border for maximum growth
compost	Any well-drained compost. In pot, JI No. 3 with extra sand or grit
care	Cut back new plants to within 15cm (6in) of the ground. Then new shoots will need supporting until aerial roots appear. Established plants can be cut hard back, leaving a few inches of the previous year's growth. Keep well-watered, particularly if in a pot as dryness at the roots will cause bud drop
propagation	Take semi-ripe 8–10cm (3–4in) cuttings in mid- to late summer. Put these in pots of cutting compost in a propagator heated to 16–21°C (61—70°F). Hardwood cuttings, 25–30cm (10–12in) long, taken in mid-autumn, will root in a cold frame
species and varieties	*C. radicans flava* has yellow trumpets. *C. grandiflora*, the Chinese trumpet vine, is larger and has rosier flowers; *C. × tagliabuana* 'Madame Galen' has pinkish-orange trumpets and more noticeably toothed leaves

ANGEL'S TRUMPETS
(Brugmansia arborea formerly *Datura)*

Daturas, or brugmansias as they have now been renamed, are a classic Victorian conservatory plant with huge soft green leaves and dramatic hanging white trumpets. They need a considerable amount of space, but, unlike swallows, one brugmansia really does make a conservatory. Watching the flower buds as they slowly elongate to nearly 15cm (6in) before they open their petals is quite awesome. Take care though: they are extremely poisonous.

category	Fragrant
type	Semi-evergreen shrub
flowers	Huge, white, flaring trumpets often more than 15cm (6in) long
leaves	Mid-green, oval with a long point
height	1.2–2.5m (4–8ft)
spread	1–1.5m (3–5ft)
temperature	4°C (39°F)
position	Light shade in summer
planting	Large pot, tub or border (where they may grow larger than stated)
compost	JI No. 2
care	Keep well-watered in summer and mist regularly if red spider mite becomes a problem. Brugmansias are fast growers and correspondingly heavy feeders. Give regular liquid feeds at 7–10 day intervals. In late winter, cut back all growth to within 15cm (6in) of ground, or grow shrub as a standard (see p.72). Repot in spring each year. They can be stood outside during the summer in a very sheltered position. Any wind will damage the large leaves
propagation	Tip cuttings in spring will root if inserted into cutting compost and kept at a temperature of 18–24°C (64–75°F). Brugmansias root very easily and it is worth trying to root any prunings during late spring and summer
species and varieties	*Brugmansia × candida* 'Grand Marnier' is a reliable yellow form. *B. sanguinea* has yellow and orange flowers; *B. suaveolens* has white trumpets

CAPE PRIMROSE
(*Streptocarpus* 'Constant Nymph')

The cape primrose flowers from midsummer to quite late on in the autumn. The tubular flowers grow in clusters on the tops of tall stems and do not look at all like primroses. It is the long, round-ended wrinkled leaves that resemble those of the primrose. For those with a deeply shaded conservatory, the cape primrose is the ideal summer-flowering plant. New hybrids are available with showy flowers in rich colours.

category	Cool and shady
type	Evergreen perennial
flowers	Blue, white-throated funnel-shaped flowers with darker veins, in small clusters
leaves	Rosettes of long, wrinkled, strap-shaped leaves
height	15–25cm (6–10in)
spread	30–40cm (12–16in)
temperature	10–15°C (50–59°F)
position	Shade
planting	13–20cm (5–8in) pots
compost	JI No. 2 or all-purpose peat-based compost
care	Water freely from early spring to mid-autumn, but keep plants only just moist during winter. Weak liquid feed every 10–14 days. Re-pot in early spring each year. Do not allow to get over-heated in summer
propagation	Many experts advise growing streptocarpus as annuals. Seed can be sown in late winter to produce autumn-flowering plants or in late spring to flower in summer the following year. Sow in pots or trays of seed compost at a temperature of 18°C (64°F). Prick out into 8cm (3in) pots. To propagate named varieties of streptocarpus, or particularly good flowering plants, it is necessary to take leaf cuttings, using either small leaves or 8cm (3in) sections of larger leaves. For additional information about leaf cuttings, see p.68
species and varieties	*S.* 'Gloria' has pink flowers. *S.* 'Kim' has deep inky-blue flowers and *S.* 'Ruby' dark red. The species *S. caulescens* has sprawling stems and small oval leaves that grow in opposite pairs. The violet-purple flowers are small and quiver on fine stems

HIBISCUS
(*Hibiscus rosa-sinensis*)

The wonderfully vivid flowers of the Chinese rose are displayed to perfection against the dark glossy foliage. A mature shrub smothered in blooms is something to strive for. However, hibiscus flower well at an early age when they are still quite small.

category	Challenging
type	Evergreen shrub
flowers	Scarlet, funnel-shaped, up to 13cm (5in) across, with a prominent long column of fused stamens
leaves	Glossy, deep green oval with serrated edges
height	1.8m (6ft)
spread	1.2m (4ft)
temperature	13–18°C (55–64°F). *H. rosa-sinensis* will survive at 4°C (39°F) but lose its leaves
position	Sun or semi-shade
planting	Grow in border to give large plants
compost	JI No. 2 or 3
care	Give a weak liquid feed at two week intervals during the growing season. To keep plants in leaf and flower all year, maintain a temperature of at least 16°C (61°F) and ensure the plants are well-watered. Low temperatures cause leaf drop, while draughts and dryness at the root cause bud drop. Plants in pots should be pruned hard back and potted on each spring until a 30cm (12in) pot is reached. Then top dress annually. In the conservatory border, keep the plant to the required size by shortening lateral shoots and leaders by a third each spring. If the plant does lose its leaves as a result of cold, keep it just moist over the winter and bring back into growth by increasing water in spring
propagation	Take 8–10cm (3–4in) heel cuttings of lateral shoots in spring or summer. Root in a cutting compost at 18°C (64°F). Transplant the rooted cuttings to 8cm (3in) pots of JI No. 2 compost. Pinch out the tips to ensure a bushy plant
species and varieties	*H. rosa-sinensis* has many cultivars including 'The President' which is bright pink and 'Nairobi' which is golden. *H. rosa-sinensis* 'Cooperi' has narrow leaves variegated with white and pink and smaller, crimson flowers. It can be grown indoors as a pot plant

Cape primrose

practical
project

MAKING A SMALL
WATER FEATURE

One way of increasing the humidity in a conservatory is to place shallow bowls of water on the ground. Making a small pond creates humidity in the same way but there is the added pleasure of growing some indoor aquatic plants. An indoor pond can be as simple or as elaborate as you please.

MAKING A BARREL POND

Planted with a small water lily and a taller growing marginal plant such as *Cyperus alternifolius*, a small water feature makes an attractive sight. Almost any watertight container can be used, but a wooden barrel is ideal. It has a pleasant, neutral appearance and the thickness of the wood prevents too much fluctuation in water temperature.

■ Choose a well-made half-barrel. Paint both the inside and the rim thickly with bitumi-

nous paint. Varnish the outside if required. Allow to dry thoroughly before adding water.

■ Allow the water to settle before planting up as shown in the illustration on p81.

MAKING A RAISED POND

The technique used is basically the same as for building a planting trough (see p.16) with a few alterations.

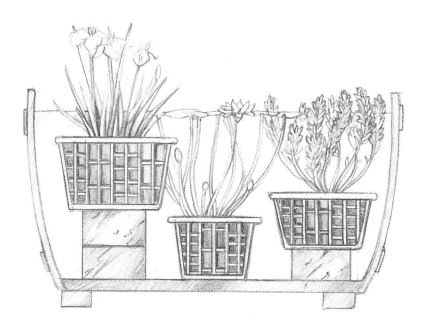

Eichornia crassipes, the water hyacinth, with spikes of blue flowers, floats on the surface of the pond buoyed up by its inflated leaf stems. It is frost tender and will survive at 1°C (34°F) but is much more successful if grown at a temperature of 27°C (80°F)

Tall-growing marginal plants that make an interesting contrast are the umberella grass, *Cyperus involucratus,* any of the many cultivars of *Iris ensata*, the Japanese iris, and *Zantedeschia rehmannii,* a pink arum lily from South Africa

YOU WILL NEED

Bricks

Sand

Cement

A pre-formed rectangular pond liner

Edging tiles

■ To make a raised pond indoors, a moulded plastic liner is recommended as there is less chance of this being punctured accidentally.

■ Follow the instructions given on p.16 for building a planting trough, adapting it to the size of the pre-purchased plastic liner and omitting the pipe that was inserted to drain away excess water.

■ Do not lay the final edging, however.

■ For double security, waterproof interior by painting it with a bituminous paint.

■ Put a thick layer of sand at the bottom and place the liner in position.

■ Make sure it is absolutely level and pack spaces with more builders' sand.

■ When the liner is in position, finish the edge of the trough, concealing the edges of the liner with flat tiles, slates or pavers.

■ You can then fill the pond with water. Allow the water to settle for some time before planting the pond.

WATER LILIES FOR SMALL PONDS

Nymphaea pygmaea 'Helvola', a tiny, pale yellow water lily is one of the best plants for a small pond
N. tetragona, white, is another miniature
N. 'Aurora', opens from cream buds, to yellow, then changes to orange and finally crimson

Although the water lilies recommended for small ponds and tubs are miniatures, small and even medium-sized varieties will adapt to life in tiny ponds by remaining smaller than they would be if given unlimited space to grow in

If an aquarium heater can be installed to raise the temperature of the pond to at least 18°C (64°F) tropical water lilies will flourish. There are blue and purple varieties as well as the whites, reds, pinks and yellows that are found among the hardier species and cultivars.

practical
project

MAKING A SMALL
WATER FEATURE
continued

FOUNTAIN FEATURE

The sound of water has a cooling effect in the conservatory. A small fountain also adds to the humidity which is very beneficial to the plants. Wall-mounted fountains that use a small submersible pump do not have to be plumbed in to the water supply. They re-circulate the water in the system although, of course, this has to be kept topped-up at all times.

Choose a low-voltage pump that connects to a transformer plugged into the mains supply. The pump can either be used to circulate water or to create a fountain jet. The fountain head can be adjusted to produce different types of spray or simply to bubble through the water.

MORE ELABORATE WATER FEATURES

The same small submersible pump can be used with an additional length of flexible pipe, to create waterfalls, cascades and grottoes.

Preformed sections are widely available and the principles are simple, as the diagram shows. The choice is yours.

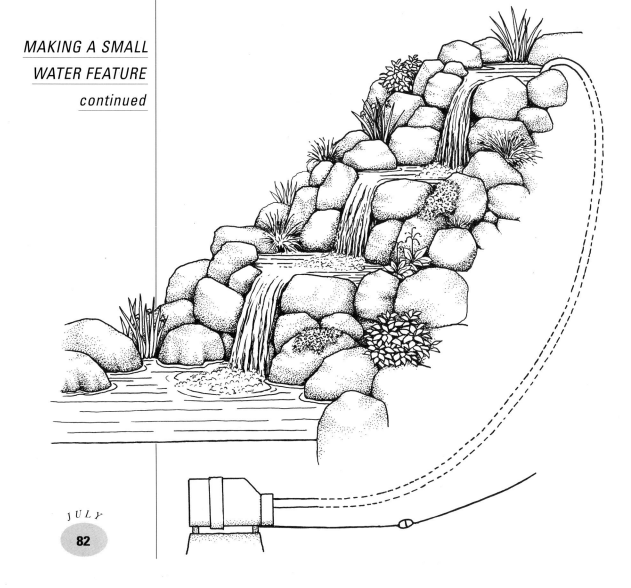

PLANTING IN WATER

■ Some perforated baskets or containers have a fine lining as part of their construction; others will have to be lined with hessian to prevent fine particles of soil from being washed out.

■ After lining, fill the pot with the soil which has had a handful or two of bone meal added. The soil should be heavy, slightly sticky, so that it does not disintegrate into separate particles in the water. Do not use peat or compost – these are too fine and light.

■ Plant the container and cover the soil with a 2.5cm (1in) layer of gravel.

■ Soak the container well before lowering it carefully into the water (not forgetting that the pond water should have been left to stand for some time before any plants are put into it).

■ The leaves of water lilies should float on the surface of the water. If they do not, support the container on a brick: this can be removed later as the leaves extend. Marginal plants will also need to be supported on bricks so that they are at the correct depth.

PLANTS FOR INDOOR WATER GARDENS

Azolla caroliniana (Fairy moss)
Cyperus involucratus (Umbrella plant)
Eichornia crassipes (Water hyacinth)
Myriophyllum aquaticum (Parrot's feather)
Nelumbo nucifera (Sacred lotus)
Zantedeschia hybrids (Arum lilies)

TROPICAL WATER LILIES
Nymphaea 'August Koch'
N. capensis hybrids
N. colorata
N. 'Director George T. Moore'
N. 'Evelyn Randig'
N. 'St. Louis Gold'

plants

OF THE

month

2

SUCCULENTS

FOR THE

CONSERVATORY

Succulent plants come into their own this month. If the conservatory is frequently unattended, it can still be kept attractive using groups of succulents and cacti which will survive neglect, drought and heat for several weeks. Display them to advantage by arranging the plants carefully on unusual stands, like the wrought-iron etagères designed to fit into corners.

The tables suggest plants for sunny and shady conservatories. Heights and spreads are approximate as so much depends on growing conditions. Many succulents are chiefly grown for their foliage and are shy to flower; any flowers should be considered a special bonus.

SUCCULENTS FOR A SUNNY CONSERVATORY

plant	colour	height and spread
Agave americana 'Variegata' (Century Plant)	Sword-shaped, green, edged cream; flowers cream	1-1.8m (3-6ft)
Crassula arborescens (Silver Jade Plant)	Rounded, silvery blue, red edges; flowers pink	4m (12ft), 2m (6ft)
Crassula ovata (Money Plant)	Rounded, bright green, sometimes red-edged; flowers white	90cm (36in), 75cm (30in)
Echeveria pulvinata (Plush Plant)	Spoon-shaped in rosettes; flowers scarlet	30cm (12in), 50cm (20in)
E. elegans	Spoon-shaped, silvery blue; flowers pink with red and yellow tips	5cm (2in), 50cm (20in)
E. harmsii	Lance shaped, glaucous blue-grey; flowers yellow, tipped red	20-30cm (8-12in), 20-25cm (8-10in)
Euphorbia milii (Crown of Thorns)	Oval, green; flowers tiny, yellow, in brilliant scarlet bracts	90cm (3ft), 45cm (18in)
Kalanchoe blossfeldiana (Flaming Katy)	Toothed, dark green, flowers yellow, pink, red, white	30cm (12in), 30cm (12in)
K. manginii	Notched olive-green; flowers red	60cm (24in)
K. 'Tessa'	Oval, olive-green; flowers pale orange	60cm (24in)
K. tubiflora	Grey-green, reddish brown mottling; flowers pale orange	1m (3ft), 30cm (1ft)
Pachyphytum oviferum (Moonstones)	Rounded, glaucous blue; flowers cream	10cm (4in), 23cm (9in)
Sedum morganium (Donkey-tail)	Trailing, palest green; flowers rose-pink, summer	60-90cm (24-36in), 30cm (12in)
S. sempervivoides	Diamond-shaped, glaucous green, marked red and purple; flowers scarlet	8-10cm (3-4in), 5cm (2in)
S. sieboldii 'Mediovariegatum'	Rounded, blue-green splashed cream; flowers pink	23cm (9in), 23cm (9in)
S. spathulifolium 'Capo Blanco'	Rosettes, blue-grey; flowers yellow	5cm (2in), indefinite
Sempervivum arachnoideum	Red-tipped green, hairy; flowers bright pink	5-12cm (2-5in), 10cm (4in) or more
Senecio rowleyanus (String of Beads)	Spherical green; flowers white	1m (3ft), indefinite

SUCCULENTS FOR A SHADY CONSERVATORY

Aeonium arboreum	Spoon-shaped in rosettes, bright green; flowers yellow	60cm (24in)
A. a. 'Atropurpureum'	Spoon-shaped in rosettes, purple; flowers white	60cm (24in)
A. a. 'Zwartkop'	Almost black rosettes	60cm (24in)
Ceropegia linearis ssp woodii (String of Hearts)	Heart-shaped, dark green overlaid with silver, purple undersides; flowers darkest maroon. It can grow into a curtain of long, trailing stems with small marbled green leaves and strange purple flowers	1-2m (3-7ft), 15-20cm (6-8in)
Crassula schmidtii	Dark green; flowers bright pink	10cm (4in), 30cm (12in)
Schlumbergera bridgesii (Christmas Cactus)	Lance-shaped, light green; flowers bright pink willl flower at Christmas if kept in a deeply shaded, unheated conservatory in summer and autumn	30cm (12in), 75cm (30in)

AUGUST

In the hot, heavy days of late summer the dramatic satiny purple flowers of Tibouchina urvilleana, *the Chilean glory flower, are guaranteed to delay anyone planning to hurry through the conservatory to the garden. Two other southern hemisphere plants are in flower now and always attract attention too, but for different reasons. The first is remarkable at the moment for its noise! The Australian hoyas are twining plants with fleshy leaves and clusters of small, velvety pink and white flowers. H. carnosa is very attractive to bees who are collecting its abundant nectar and their loud, satisfied humming is quite memorable. The unusual flowers of* Mirabilis jalapa *(marvel of Peru) are randomly coloured mixtures of pink, white and yellow. However, it is their evening perfume that stops visitors in their tracks. If grown inside they will flower the same year from seed, and you can save the tubers of plants with the most exciting multicoloured flowers for the following year.*

Watering of camellias and azaleas is still essential but as the level of rainwater in the water-butt is continually diminishing and not being topped up, save cool, boiled water from the kettle and the remains in the teapot for essential uses. Correas, leptospermums, boronias and citrus fruits also need soft water. Keep them in the shade and mulch the top with gravel to prevent evaporation from the surface of the pot.

A shady conservatory well-furnished with foliage plants is at its most enticing on a hot day. The varied leaves of begonias and the fronds of ferns and palms make a lively, textured background for the many flowers that appreciate coolness in summer. Streptocarpus are well worth investigating for this situation. There are interesting species like
S. candidus *with small white flowers, or the small-leaved*
S. caulescens *with single purple flowers that dance on the end of narrow stems* (see p.79). *Fuchsias are flourishing in the shade and warmth too, with even more varieties, species and sizes to choose from.*

CHECKLIST

- Take cuttings
- Plant tender bulbs, corms and tubers
- Plan for winter fragrance
- Repair and maintain

tasks

FOR THE

month

SPRING-FLOWERING DWARF BULBS

Now is the time to send off for bulb catalogues and order a variety of spring-flowering dwarf bulbs for the conservatory. Try some of the following :

Chionodoxa
Crocus
Hyacinth
Iris
Muscari
Narcissus
Scilla
Snowdrop
Tulip

Prepared hyacinth and narcissus bulbs will be on sale at the end of the month. Plant some in pots for Christmas

EASY CUTTINGS

One of the easiest ways of making more plants is by rooting cuttings in jars of water at this time of year. It is worth trying to propagate any of the following plants during the period in which they are in full growth: fuchsias, geraniums, *Streptocarpus* species, coleus, ivy, tradescantia, philodendron, *Rhoicissus* species, impatiens (Busy lizzies), chlorophytum, *Saintpaulia* (African violets), *Begonia semperflorens* and peperomia.

■ Take a healthy shoot about 8cm (3in) long and remove the lower leaves.

■ Place a small piece of wire netting over the mouth of a clear glass jar and bend it over the sides of the jar to hold in place. Thread the cuttings through the wire and put it in a light, warm place but out of direct sunlight.

■ Keep the water level constant and replace it if it becomes discoloured.
■ The roots produced in this way are very fine and care must be taken when potting them up.

■ Use a soft peat-based potting compost and handle them gently by the leaves. As with all soft cuttings, care must be taken not to bruise the stems.

■ The trailing blue or white campanula, *C. isophylla*, roots easily if bits are pulled off and inserted in some potting compost.

■ Pelargonium cuttings, taken just below a node with a sharp knife, root easily in well-drained sandy compost.

TENDER BULBS, CORMS AND TUBERS

These are some of the prettiest flowers for the conservatory; they are easy and will frequently flower a few months after planting.
Lachenalias, the Cape cowslips, should be planted now for a long flowering season. *L. aloides* var. *aurea* has golden-yellow flowers, and *L.a.* var. *quadricolor* has spikes

of purplish buds which open to red and yellow. Put six bulbs 2.5cm (1in) deep in a 13cm (5in) clay pot of JI No. 2 compost mixed with the same amount of general-purpose peat-based compost and some extra grit and sand. Keep in a cool place. Lachenalias can also be displayed in a hanging basket. Line it well with moss, use the same compost and plant the bulbs to grow from the bottom and sides as well as the top.

Freesias for Christmas flowering should be planted now in the same way.

Veltheimia bracteata, like a small, pink red-hot poker, should be planted in clay pots with the tips of the bulbs just showing above the soil surface. It needs good light and well-drained compost.

Hippeastrums should be planted with half the bulb showing above the compost surface (see also p.133).

If zantedeschias (arum or calla lilies) have been more than a year in their pots, they should be repotted and started into growth. Shake off the old compost and replant in JI No. 2 with some bone meal added. They may have made offsets, in which case these can be removed and potted up separately. Water sparingly at first but more generously as the leaves grow. Zantedeschias need to be kept at a temperature of 13°C (55°F) if they are to flower in the winter.

■ Seeds of the many different cultivars of *Cyclamen persicum* can be sown now. Sowing this month produces large plants which will flower in fifteen months. Some new varieties should flower more quickly.

■ Soak the seed in hot water for twenty-four hours.

■ Then sow the seeds very thinly in JI seed compost and germinate out-of-doors in a cool place where a

temperature of between 13–16°C (55–61°F) is required. (Higher temperatures inhibit germination.)

■ Prick out the seedlings into 6.5cm (2½in) pots of JI No. 1 when they have two leaves and keep them at 16°C (61°F).

■ In late spring, pot them on into 9cm (3½in) pots of JI No. 2, and later, into their final 13cm (5in) pots.

WINTER FRAGRANCE

Brompton stocks, *Matthiola incana*, and mignonette, *Reseda odorata*, can be sown now to provide scented pot plants for the winter.

■ The seed of the Brompton stocks can be sown outside in nursery rows from early summer to the beginning of the month. Thin the plants to 15cm (6in) apart. Pot them up in early autumn into JI No. 2 in 15cm (6in) pots and keep them at a temperature of between 10–13°C (50–55°F). Water regularly and apply a liquid feed when the buds appear.

■ Sow a scattered pinch of *Reseda odorata* seed in a 13cm (5in) pot of JI No. 1. Thin out to the strongest three seedlings. When they are growing strongly, pinch out the tops to make the plants bush out.

■ Wallflowers sown in late spring/early summer should be pricked out to 15cm (6in) apart. In early autumn pot them up like Brompton stocks and let them stand outside until midwinter.

REPAIR AND MAINTENANCE

The conservatory should be thoroughly cleaned at a time when as many plants as

possible can be taken outside, and perhaps left there overnight without any danger of frost.

■ First remove all the rubbish, then sweep any surfaces.

■ Wash down the conservatory framework with a disinfectant recommended for the purpose, using a brush to get into all the cracks.

■ Clean the windows inside and outside. A long-handled mop will be necessary for the roof and squeegees save time. Overlapping sections of glass will need to be cleaned by inserting a piece of thin card to scrape away the green algae. Old playing cards are ideal for this task!

■ Gravel or other material in the gravel trays should be washed in a sieve. Sand that has become mixed with soil in the propagating bench should be replaced. Consider covering it with a layer of perforated growing film to allow warmth and moisture out but deter the roots from growing in.

■ Whilst cleaning, inspect the structure for any problems. The humidity in a conservatory is higher than other rooms in the house, and hinges, door fittings and other metal pieces may be rusting. Wood should be examined for signs of rot.

■ Check the outside gutterings and drainpipes.

■ Clean the tracks of sliding doors.

■ Oil the working parts of ventilators and louvres.

■ Wash any fabric or plastic venetian blinds.

■ Make sure that all plant pots are clean when you bring them back in, and that all the dead flowers, leaves and other debris have been removed from both plants and pots.

ROUTINE TASKS

Keep the conservatory well ventilated. Check that the temperature is not falling below 16°C (61°F) at night. If it is, close the rooflights in the evenings

Continue to water and liquid feed plants in bloom or in full growth

Achimenes, begonias, gloxinias and *Amaryllis belladonna* may have finished flowering. If so, begin gradually to reduce the watering. The tubers need to ripen and then rest

Towards the end of the month shading can be removed

Check that you have enough pots and compost

Feed grape vines with high potash feed like tomato fertilizer

Reduce watering of melon when fruit starts to ripen

Pot on rooted strawberry runners, but leave the pots outside until midwinter

Dead head regularly

Tidiness and routine hygiene are always important

HALF-HARDY ANNUALS FOR SPRING FLOWERING

Seeds of nemesia, phlox, clarkia, primula, salpiglossis, larkspur and sweet scabious can all be sown at the beginning of the month for a magnificent display next spring. Maintain a temperature of 16–18°C (61–64°F) and after germination, pot the seedlings into JI No. 2. Seeds of *Primula* × *kewensis*, *P. malacoides*, *P. obconica*, and *P. sinensis* need some light to germinate. These are all perennials but the last three are usually grown as annuals

plants
OF THE
month

 GLORY BUSH
(Tibouchina urvilleana)

This is an exotic shrub from Chile with striking royal-purple flowers and beautiful leaves as well. It is not at all demanding with regard to temperature, but needs careful pruning to keep it compact.

category	Challenging
type	Evergreen shrub
flowers	Dramatic purple flowers with a velvety sheen, each 8–10cm (3–4in) wide
leaves	Velvety, oval and up to 15cm (6in) long
height	2–3m (6½–10ft)
spread	1m (3ft)
temperature	7–10°C (45–50°F)
position	Good light but shade from hottest sun
planting	Border or large tub 46cm (18in) diameter
compost	Well-drained ericaceous compost
care	Water well from spring to end of autumn and give liquid feed every fortnight from early summer to mid-autumn. High humidity in the growing season. The shrub can grow tall and straggly. In spring, cut back flowering stems to two pairs of buds to prevent this. Reducing water and temperature will encourage the plant to rest during winter and so prolong its life. It will flower continuously at a temperature of 13–16°C (55–61°F)
propagation	Take soft or semi-ripe cuttings in late spring or summer and insert them in warmed compost at 24°C (75°F). Prune out the growing tips when the cuttings are growing well, to encourage the plant to bush out
species and varieties	*T. organensis* is less vigorous but has larger flowers; *T.* 'Jules' is a miniature version which is covered with small electric-blue flowers in summer and autumn

 HOYA
(Hoya carnosa)

A hoya always provokes comment. They do not produce leaves until there is a fair length of naked stem waving around the conservatory and the umbels of flowers look as if they have petals cut out of pink velvet and are frequently bejewelled with drops of crystal nectar. In the summer, the plant is alive with humming bees. It is an easy plant to care for, positively preferring neglect.

category	Easy
type	Evergreen climber
flowers	Hanging clusters of fragrant, star-shaped, palest pink flowers with deep pink centres
leaves	Fleshy, ovate, deep green
height	5m (16½ft) or more
temperature	5–7°C (41–45°F)
position	Indirect sun
planting	Thrive when pot-bound
compost	Prefer a slightly acid, coarse, growing medium. Add grit and leafmould to an ericaceous compost
care	Water well when in bud but hardly at all in winter. Do not repot often. A humid atmosphere is beneficial. The stems can be trained up a wall, round doors and windows or round a wire frame
propagation	Take 8–10cm (3–4in) cuttings of mature stems in summer and insert in equal parts sand and peat at a temperature of 16–18°C (61–64°F)
species and varieties	*H. carnosa* 'Variegata' has cream margins to the leaves. *H. lanceolata* subsp. *bella* is a smaller version that can be used as a hanging basket plant

MARVEL OF PERU

(Mirabilis jalapa)

Compact and floriferous plants of *Mirabilis jalapa* grow freely in cracks in walls and pavements in Greece. In a conservatory here, however, they can grow rather lax with the flowers hidden among large leaves. Copy the conditions they seem to enjoy and give them full sun and poor soil. The multicoloured flowers open for afternoon tea and release their strong perfume all evening.

category	Fragrant
type	Tuberous perennial
flowers	Small trumpet-shaped, can be yellow, deep rose-pink or white or any combination of the three, stripes, freckles or halves of the flower in different colours
leaves	Mid-green, oval
height	46–120cm (18–48in)
spread	46–60cm (18–24in)
temperature	4°C (39°F)
position	Full sun
planting	23cm (9in) pot or border
compost	Well-drained, low nutrient, Jl No. 1 with added grit and sand
care	A too-rich soil results in luxuriant foliage and a large plant that needs supporting. Water regularly from late spring to early autumn. Dry off pots as foliage dies down. The tubers can be stored in a frost-free place over winter and repotted in the following spring. If the tuber is in the border, reduce watering during winter
propagation	Plants seed freely. Sow seed in mid-spring at a temperature 21–24°C (70–75°F)

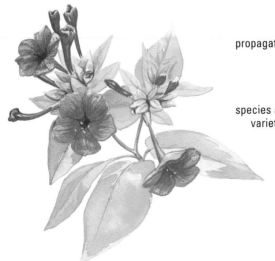

BEGONIA

(Begonia sutherlandii)

It would be possible to fill a conservatory with nothing but different begonias so diverse is the family, in flower colour, leaf, size and habit. *B. sutherlandii* is an unusual species begonia with red stems and orange flowers. It grows well in a hanging basket and resembles a pretty crinoline of leaves and flowers.

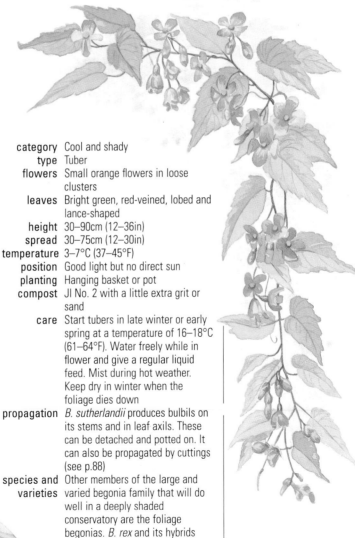

category	Cool and shady
type	Tuber
flowers	Small orange flowers in loose clusters
leaves	Bright green, red-veined, lobed and lance-shaped
height	30–90cm (12–36in)
spread	30–75cm (12–30in)
temperature	3–7°C (37–45°F)
position	Good light but no direct sun
planting	Hanging basket or pot
compost	Jl No. 2 with a little extra grit or sand
care	Start tubers in late winter or early spring at a temperature of 16–18°C (61–64°F). Water freely while in flower and give a regular liquid feed. Mist during hot weather. Keep dry in winter when the foliage dies down
propagation	*B. sutherlandii* produces bulbils on its stems and in leaf axils. These can be detached and potted on. It can also be propagated by cuttings (see p.88)
species and varieties	Other members of the large and varied begonia family that will do well in a deeply shaded conservatory are the foliage begonias. *B. rex* and its hybrids have heart-shaped leaves in combinations of green, silver, wine-red, purple, pink and rose. *B. scharffii* can grow to 1.5m (5ft) and has olive-green leaves with a red under-surface and red stems

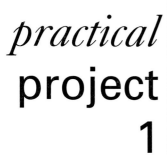

practical project 1

MAKING SLATTED STAGING

This is very sturdy shelving that will take the weight of a damp, sand-filled propagating tray (see Project of the Month p.136) and other heavy pots. It can be any convenient width and height and up to 1.8m (6ft) long.

YOU WILL NEED

Saw, Drill, Screwdriver, Carriage bolts, Screws, Timber connectors, Galvanized nails
Small-headed nails for finishing
Wood preservative
Timber, as follows:
- *Six pieces of 50 x 25mm (2 x 1in) softwood for cross rails (which should each be 200mm (8in) shorter than the overall width of the staging)*
- *Two pieces of 50 x 25mm (2 x 1in) softwood for long rails (up to 1.8m (6ft) long)*
- *Two pieces of 50 x 25mm (2 x 1in) softwood for diagonals (cut to fit)*
- *Six pieces of 50 x 50mm (2 x 2in) softwood for the legs*
- *38 x 16mm (1¹/₂ x ⁵/₈in) softwood battens to make the slatted top*
- *One 16 x 16mm (⁵/₈ x ⁵/₈in) softwood batten to finish off the top (up to 1.8m (6ft) long)*

CONSTRUCTION

- Cut cross rails and the legs to the width and height required.

- Fix the cross rails to the legs using 4cm (1¹/₂in) timber connectors and 9cm (3¹/₂in) carriage bolts. The top cross rails should be fixed level with the top of the legs and the bottom rails 5cm (2in) from the bottom.

- Prepare the long rails and using 50mm screws, screw them to the outside top of the legs.

- The next step is to measure the diagonals from 50 x 25mm (2 x 1in) timber and make bird's mouth joints at each end so that they can be screwed to the top and bottom cross rails.

- The top is made from strips of 38 x 16mm (1¹/₂ x ⁵/₈in) timber. They should be set 25mm (1in) apart and each one should over-hang the front of the frame by 4cm (1¹/₂in) in front and by 10cm (4in) at the back.

- Nail them in firmly with the galvanized nails and then finish off the front with strips of 16 x 16mm (⁵/₈ x ⁵/₈in) timber. Use small-headed nails to attach this.

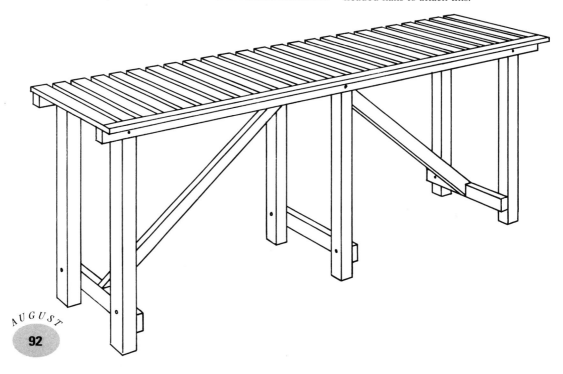

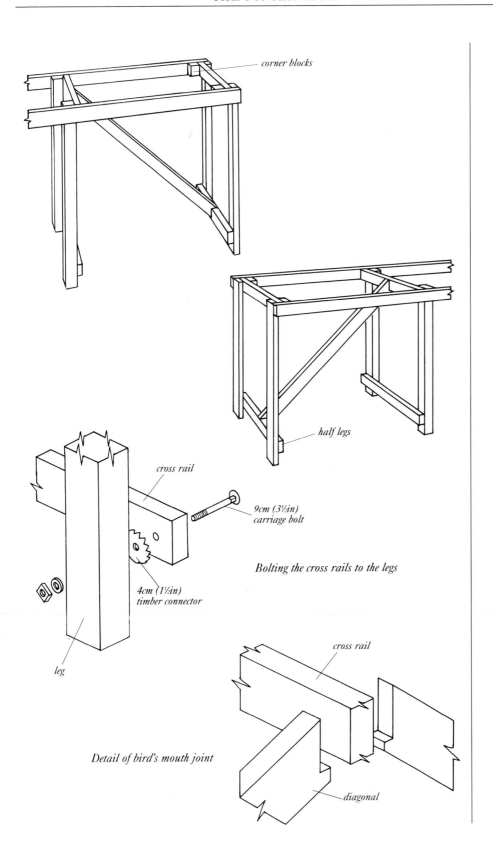

corner blocks

half legs

cross rail

9cm (3½in)
carriage bolt

Bolting the cross rails to the legs

4cm (1½in)
timber connector

leg

cross rail

Detail of bird's mouth joint

diagonal

practical
project
2

CONSTRUCTING
DISPLAY SHELVES

These shelves differ from ordinary shelves by being different widths and having a raised lip to conceal what may be a variety of different plant containers.

YOU WILL NEED

Cross-cut saw, Tenon saw
Chisel, Drill
Screwdriver, Hammer
Wood glue, Screws, Nails, Preservative
Timber, as follows:

■ *Three pieces 19 x 44mm (³/₄ x 1³/₄in) softwood, 1200mm (4ft) long for facing (or wider if required)*

■ *Six pieces 32 x 95mm (1³/₈ x 3³/₄in) softwood, 1200mm (4ft) long for the shelves*

■ *Four pieces 44 x 44mm (1³/₄ x 1³/₄in) softwood, 1200mm (4ft) long for the frame*

■ *One piece 12 x 44mm (¹/₂ x 1³/₄in), 1500mm (5ft) long for a diagonal brace*

■ The 44 x 44mm (1³/₄ x 1³/₄in) timber provides the outer supports. Two pieces lie vertically against the wall and the other two lean diagonally against them so that there is a space of 38cm (15in) at the bottom.

■ Lay the pieces down and arrange them so that you can mark and cut the angles at the top.

■ Then join the two pairs together with glue and screws.

■ When the pieces are together, decide where you want your three shelves and what distance apart you would like them to be. Measure the length for the shelf supports.

■ Cut the 19 x 44mm (³/₄ x 1³/₄in) wood into three equal pairs according to your measurements.

■ Glue and screw these to the legs.

■ Screw the boards into the rails. The lower shelf will need three widths, the second two and the top, only one.

■ Then add facings which can be nailed or screwed on.

■ The diagonal brace at the back provides extra strength and can be dovetail jointed, screwed or simply nailed.

■ The shelves can then be painted or stained with a non-toxic preservative.

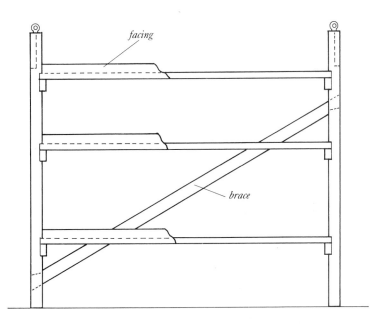

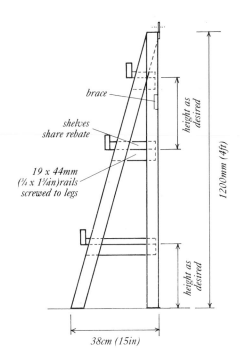

SEPTEMBER

Although it can often still seem like summer, this month is the time to remove any shading in the conservatory and think about winter. An unheated conservatory may need insulating against frost penetration. Although the days can be as warm as before, the nights become damper and cooler this month. Windows can be left open at night (and should be if the conservatory contains grapes, chrysanthemums or peach trees) but beware, for the conservatory has suddenly become a Mecca for snails and some way of keeping them out has to be devised.

If thinking about the onset of winter is depressing, planning even further ahead is a much more cheerful occupation. Now is a good time to buy bulbs and seeds for the conservatory for flowering displays early next spring. Bulbs from a reliable source are guaranteed to flower and the choice increases each year. With a conservatory, tender bulbs can be grown as well as hardy bulbs and both types have their places and flowering seasons. For early spring, look out for corms of Cyclamen pseudibericum, *a scented, bright carmine cyclamen, or the yellow muscari,* M. macrocarpum, *which is also fragrant. For a heady perfume that will fill the conservatory, hyacinths are hard to beat and now is the time to buy them.*

Many favourite conservatory and glasshouse flowers remain in full bloom. China-blue Plumbago auriculata *is flowering strongly while* Passiflora racemosa, *one of the hardier passion flowers, with hanging racemes of deep rose-pink flowers, is still in bloom, as is* Mirabilis jalapa. *Two smaller plants that are worth growing are also at their best now.* Campanula isophylla, *a trailing bellflower with silver leaves, is very reliable and so easy to propagate that after two years you could have baskets of it, indoors and out.* Kohleria 'Hanna Roberts' *is very intriguing, with small pink trumpets that open out into five spotted petals. The kohlerias are gesneriads like streptocarpus and sinningias and need similar conditions.*

tasks
FOR THE
month

PLUNGE BED
A plunge bed is a frame or specially prepared part of the ground filled with ashes, sand, gravel or peat where pots can be sunk up to their rims. This protects the roots of the plants from extremes of temperature and keeps them from drying out. Alternatively, if you don't have room for a bed, you could use a large container, such as a half-barrel as shown below

CHECKLIST

- Provide insulation
- Sow spring-flowering annuals
- Plant spring-flowering bulbs
- Plant lilies

INSULATION

The nights are longer and colder and it is a good time to prepare to insulate the conservatory if it is not double-glazed.

■ Excluding draughts is one of the simplest ways of keeping the cold out but if it is done *too* well, the air can become stagnant and this can exacerbate fungal diseases. Extra care will be necessary with ventilating the conservatory.

■ If you plan to use bubble polythene to line the conservatory, measure how much is needed and buy it now. Lining the glass roof is worth doing because that will not affect the appearance of the conservatory dramatically. Make sure you have enough clips or screws to fix it on.

■ Finally, check the heating system if you have one. Consider buying a thermostatically controlled fan heater. These can be set very low, just above freezing or at whatever is the lowest temperature your plants will survive at. The movement of air is also beneficial.

SPRING-FLOWERING ANNUALS

To ensure a succession of flowers, seeds of some plants should be sown at different times. More seed of cineraria and schizanthus can be sown this month. Other annual garden plants that make good pot plants are nigella, *Linaria maroccana* 'Fairy Bouquet', phacelia, *Mimulus* 'Calypso' F1 Hybrids, dwarf sweet peas, centaurea, calendula, *Asperula orientalis* and annual lavatera. Sown now, these will make large plants that will flower from early spring until early summer.

■ Sow seed thinly in JI seed compost and germinate in a cold frame, or in a propagator with very gentle heat.

■ When the seedlings are big enough to handle, they should be pricked out into 8cm (3in) pots of JI No. 1 and left outside.

■ Pot them on when necessary into 11cm (4½in) pots and then to 15cm (6in) pots.

■ They will need to be protected from frost, and brought indoors into a cold conservatory in early winter.

SPRING-FLOWERING BULBS

Hardy spring-flowering bulbs should be planted as early as possible this month. Dwarf and miniature narcissi and crocuses should be planted first, then irises, hyacinths, early tulips, ixias, gladioli and the bulbous-rooted irises. These can all be planted in pots (as well as in garden borders) to give colour to the conservatory in early spring.

There is still time to plant lachenalias, freesias, *Veltheimia bracteata* and zantedeschias as described last month. Add to these nerines, *Cyrtanthus purpureus*, the Scarborough lily, and cyclamen corms.

Bulbs will grow happily in bulb fibre for one season but if they are to last and increase over the years, a compost that contains nutrients is necessary. This can be made from 2 parts peat (or peat substitute), 3 parts coarse grit and 4 parts loam, together with a fertilizer base or bone meal at 28g (1oz) weight to 4.5 litres (1 gallon) by bulk. Unless the compost is needed for lime-hating plants, add 7g (¼oz) lime to the mixture. More simply, add one-third sand and grit, by bulk, to JI No. 2 compost.

■ Plant each bulb at a depth that is between two or three times the bulb's length and with at least 2.5cm (1in) of compost underneath.

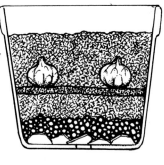

■ Most bulbs should also be planted one bulb's width distance from another. Narcissi, however, can be more closely planted.

■ If possible, use clay pots for bulbs that like hot conditions such as nerines, and the watsonias which come from South Africa, and plastic for 'woodland' bulbs like snowdrops, corydalis and trilliums.

■ Plant each bulb at a depth that is between two or three times the bulb's length and with at least 2.5cm (1in) of compost underneath.

■ Most bulbs should also be planted one bulb's width distance from another. Narcissi, however, can be more closely planted.

■ When the bulbs have been potted, the pots should be put in a dark, cool place for eight weeks to encourage good root growth. A frost-free cellar or garage can be used.

■ Otherwise, the pots can be kept out-of-doors in a 'plunge' bed or covered with a thick layer (at least 8cm/3in) of peat, coconut fibre, forest bark, sifted ashes or sand.

Plant ixias five or seven to a 15cm (6in) pot, 8cm (3in) deep for a spring and early summer display. Bring them into the cool conservatory when the shoots appear. They need water, good light and cool conditions. *Iris danfordiae* and crocus, providing they do not freeze solid in their containers, can be left out-of-doors and should only be brought in when the shoots are 5cm (2in) high.

LILIES

Lilies are always elegant and many are heavily scented too. One or two pots of lilies can transform a conservatory

overnight and are well worth the advance planning. They are very prone to drying out and if possible the best thing to do is to buy bulbs that have just become dormant, and replant them immediately.

Lilies need a good depth of rich soil and sharp drainage. Prepare deep roots with crocks and gravel at the bottom, then a layer of leafmould and finish off with JI No. 2 compost with

added grit and sand. *L. martagon* and other stem-rooting lilies should be planted 5cm (2in) above the drainage crock, to allow room for the roots to grow from the stems. A 15cm (6in) plant pot holds three small bulbs of *L. pumilum* or one medium-size bulb such as *L.* 'Enchantment'. The very large bulb of *L. auratum* will need a 20cm (8in) pot and an acid compost. (See p.59.)

PROPAGATING LILIES

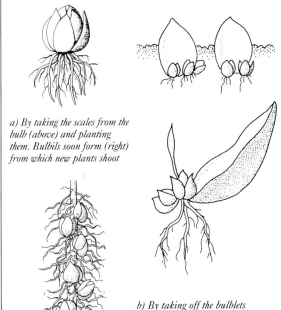

a) By taking the scales from the bulb (above) and planting them. Bulbils soon form (right) from which new plants shoot

b) By taking off the bulblets that form on the buried part of the stem and planting them

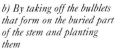

c) By taking off the bulbils that form in the leaf axils and planting them

ROUTINE TASKS

Remove all shading

Check heating system, if any

Protect grapes from wasps

Reduce frequency of watering. Do not water in late evening unless temperatures remain high

Continue to feed pot plants but change to high potash feed which will help the stems to ripen

Buy lily bulbs if possible. Basal-rooting lilies can be planted in pots now

Bring in late-flowering chrysanthemums. If the weather is unusally cold, or you live in a cold area, you may need to bring in azaleas, solanum, camellias and citrus trees now

Prick out and pot on plants that are ready. Any primulas and calceolarias that were sown in mid-spring should be ready for final, 13cm (5in) pots. Primulas sown in early summer will need to go into 8cm (3in) pots. Schizanthus sown last month will need pricking out. Allow the plants plenty of room. At the end of the month, cyclamen seed sown in late summer will need pricking out or potting – wait until they have two or three leaves each

STEM-ROOTING LILIES

L auratum
L henryi
L longiflorum
L pumilum
L regale
L formosanum
L 'Enchantment'

plants

OF THE

month

1

 FATSIA
(*Fatsia japonica*)

Fatsia makes a fine dramatic backbone plant for the conservatory. The large glossy leaves make a good contrast to the flimsier leaves of many of the flowering plants. A well-grown fatsia looks good all year round.

category	Easy
type	Evergreen shrub
flowers	Clusters of tiny white flowers, like those of the ivy, are followed by black berries
leaves	Large, palmate with 7–9 lobes or 'fingers', deep green
height	3m (10ft)
spread	3m (10ft)
temperature	0°C (32°F)
position	Sun or shade
planting	13–18cm (5–7in) pots at first. Transfer to border or large tub when necessary
compost	JI No. 2
care	Repot annually in early spring
propagation	Seed can be sown in spring at a temperature of 10–13°C (50–55°F). Prick out seedlings into 8cm (3in) pots of JI No. 1. Semi-ripe cuttings can be taken in summer or suckers detached and potted up as for the seedlings
species and varieties	*F. japonica* 'Variegata' has creamy white margins and is slightly more tender

CHILEAN BELLFLOWER
(*Lapageria rosea*)

The large waxen blooms, pink, white or sometimes slightly chequered, of the Chilean bellflower make it one of the most desirable conservatory plants. It is quite difficult to create the conditions for it to flourish, however.

category	Challenging
type	Evergreen climber
flowers	8cm (3in) hanging deep pink bells with thick sheeny petals
leaves	Pointed oval, leathery, dark green
height	3–4.5m (10–15ft)
temperature	7°C (45°F); cool in summer – maximum 21°C (70°F)
position	Cool, shaded from hot sun in summer
planting	Very large pot or border. Allow plant to twine round trellis (not wires which may get too hot) and across roof
compost	Ericaceous compost

care	Lapagerias like a very even temperature and must be kept cool and moist at the roots. Water well in summer and keep the humidity high. Give a liquid feed from late spring to later summer. Good ventilation is essential. Greenfly, slugs, mealy bug and scale insect can all be troublesome. Prune to fit space in early spring
propagation	If lapageria sets seed, this should be sown as soon as possible in seed compost at a temperature of between 13–18°C (55–64°F). Or take semi-ripe cuttings in early summer. Strong shoots can be layered in mid- to late spring or in late autumn
species and varieties	*L. rosea* var. *albiflora* has white flowers; there is a pale pink variety called *L. rosea* 'Flesh Pink', and another, *L. rosea* 'Nash Court', which is a soft, marbled pink

PICK-A-BACK PLANT
(*Tolmeia menziesii* 'Taff's Gold')

This is another good-tempered foliage plant. It forms compact clumps of rough, bright leaves and makes good 'ground' cover beneath larger specimens.

category	Easy
type	Evergreen perennial
flowers	Small bell-shaped, greenish flowers in spikes
leaves	Ivy-shaped, hairy, mid-green splashed with gold
height	15cm (6in), with flower stems up to 46cm (18in)
spread	30–40cm (12–16in)
temperature	0°C (32°F)
position	Shade or sun
planting	10–13cm (4–5in) pots

compost	JI No. 2
care	Repot annually in spring and water freely while in growth
propagation	Detach the leaves and the young plantlets that form at the base and pot them up in JI No. 1 compost in seed trays or individual 8cm (3in) pots
species and varieties	*T. menziesii* has attravtive green leaves

▲ ARABIAN JASMINE
(*Jasminum sambac* 'Maid of Orleans')

This deliciously scented twining yet bushy jasmine will flower almost continuously if the temperature is high enough. The semi-double white flowers fade prettily to wine-red.

category	Fragrant
type	Evergreen climber
flowers	White, small, in threes, highly fragrant
leaves	In opposite pairs, slightly hairy
height	1.5–3m (5–10ft)
spread	1–1.8m (3–6ft)
temperature	7–10°C (45–50°F) minimum
position	Sun or partial shade
planting	25–30cm (10–12in) pot or border
compost	JI No. 2
care	Will need to be supported on canes, wires or a pillar. Water freely in summer
propagation	Take heel cuttings 8–10cm (3–4in) long and insert into a cutting compost with bottom heat of 16°C (61°F). When they have rooted, pot each one into an 8cm (3in) pot of JI No. 2 compost. Pinch out growing tips
species and varieties	*J. sambac* 'Grand Duke of Tuscany' has slightly frilly double flowers which fade to deep maroon. It is also bushy but larger and difficult to keep tidy

GLOXINIA ▶
(*Sinningia speciosa* hybrids)

The popular gloxinias that are available in rich red, violets, whites and pinks, often speckled or with contrasting white edges, have all been developed from *Sinningia speciosa*. They make a wonderful display.

category	Cool and shady
type	Tuberous perennial
flowers	Wide bells in rich colours, 5–8cm (2–3in) across
leaves	Rich velvety green. Can be 30cm (12in) long and 12cm (5in) wide
height	To 46cm (18in)
spread	30cm (12in)
temperature	10°C (50°F). In summer, 18°C (64°F)
position	Shade
planting	In late winter, place the tubers in moist peat and start into growth at a temperature of 21°C (70°F). When the shoots are 2.5–5cm (1–2in) high, pot up tubers separately into 13–15cm (5–6in) pots
compost	JI No. 2 or all-purpose peat or peat substitute compost
care	Give plants a liquid feed every seven to ten days from the time of the first flower bud to the last flower. Keep plants humid and well watered. Gradually cease watering as leaves turn yellow. Store tubers in a dry place over winter to use again the following year
propagation	Sow seeds in late winter or early spring in JI seed compost at a temperature of 21°C (70°F). Prick out seedlings when second leaves appear into 6cm (2½in) pots of JI No. 2 or the alternative and after a few days, lower the temperature to 18°C (64°F). Pot on as necessary. In mid-spring tubers can be divided. Each piece should have a shoot on it and can then be potted up into 8cm (3in) pots in the compost. Otherwise, take 5–8cm (2–3in) long basal cuttings of shoots with a thin segment of the tuber attached. Pot up as before
species and varieties	*S. speciosa* 'Mont Blanc' is pure white; *S. speciosa* 'Duchess of York', purple with a white edge. *Sinningia regina* is smaller, with white-veined leaves and violet-purple flowers

practical project

FRUIT IN THE CONSERVATORY

RECOMMENDED GRAPE VINES

For an unheated conservatory, one of the Sweetwater grapes, which ripens early, is the easiest choice. The fruits are juicy and sweet with thin skins. They do not keep. *Vitis* 'Black Hamburgh' (now called *V.* 'Schiava Grossa'), is a reliable variety. *V.* 'Buckland Sweetwater' is a white grape that is also recommended for a cool conservatory. Both of these do well in pots

OTHER RECOMMENDED VARIETIES

BLACK GRAPES:
Muscats
'Cardinal'
'Madeira Frontignan'
Sweetwater
'Black Prince'
Vinous
'Alicante'
'Gros Colmar'

WHITE GRAPES:
Muscats
'Royal Muscadine'
'Muscat d'Alexandria'
Sweetwater
'Chasselan Vibert'
Vinous
'Golden Queen'
'Syrian'

Classic greenhouse crops like grapes, peaches, apricots, oranges and lemons can be grown for their fruit in the conservatory and they are all ornamental as well. However, if they are to fruit successfully, they must be kept cool at certain times when the people using the conservatory might prefer to be warm! Grape vines, citrus fruits and peaches all need a certain amount of winter chilling and this will restrict the choice of other plants.

The conservatory is also the ideal place for forcing strawberries.

GRAPES IN POTS

Ideally, grapes should be grown on the back wall in a border or large planting trough, or with the roots outside the conservatory and the vine inside. One of the advantages of this month's project is that the pots can be moved outside for a period, to be chilled.

Container-grown vines are available at any time of the year. Grape vines also root very easily and you might be able to persuade someone to pass on some of their prunings. It is usually best to plant the canes in the winter when they should be firmly staked.

YOU WILL NEED

Grape vine: Two-year-old canes are the cheapest
30cm (12in) pot
JI No. 3 potting compost
Bamboo cane
Secateurs

■ While the vine is dormant, cut back the stem to a strong bud 15cm (6in) from the ground.

■ When growth starts in the spring, one leader should be tied to the cane. This leader will produce side shoots or laterals which should be stopped by pruning off the growing tip when five or six leaves have been produced.

■ Reduce any sub-laterals (shoots that are growing from the laterals) to one leaf.

■ The grape vine should not be allowed to

bear fruit until it is three years old, so any flowers that appear must be picked off.

■ The following winter, the new growth of the leader should be reduced by two-thirds, down to well-ripened wood.

■ The laterals should be cut back to one bud each.

■ In the summer, tie in the leading shoot and prune as for summer the first year.

■ The third winter's pruning is the same as before. The one strong bud that has been left on the laterals will produce the fruiting shoots.

■ Every year, from then on, two fruiting shoots are allowed at each lateral and the rest pinched out.

Routine care
■ Water well during the growing season.

■ It may be necessary to hand-pollinate the flower trusses. Do this by shaking the plant a little or running your hand over the truss.

■ Keep very well ventilated at all times. If it is very hot, extra humidity must be provided by damping down the floor. (See p.68.)

GRAPE VINE FOR A TABLE DECORATION

If you have an established vine, you might consider one of the techniques that the Victorians used to provide small pots of fruiting grapes as table decorations, as described by Ray Waite, Superintendent of the Glasshouses at the Royal Horticultural Society's Garden, Wisley.

■ In late winter, take a vigorous shoot of the previous year and pass the tip through the hole in the bottom of a 20cm (8in) clay pot to a maximum length of 60cm (24in) to the top of the compost.

■ Fill the pot with JI No. 3 potting compost and firm it down. Leave space at the top for watering.

■ You will need to devise a way of supporting the pot at that level. A cane of this length will have four or five buds on it. Support the stem by tying it to a short, thick bamboo cane.

HAND-POLLINATE FRUIT

Peaches, nectarines, apricots, strawberries and grapes in bloom will need hand-pollinating this month. You will need a soft artist's paint brush to transfer the pollen from the anthers of one blossom to

the stigma of another. Move dry pollen from one blossom to another at midday for several days running

■ Remove any shoots that appear from below the compost and pinch out the ones above to two leaves beyond any flower truss that forms. If there are no flowers, leave the shoots with five leaves.

■ The bunches of developing grapes will need thinning.

■ When the fruit has ripened, gradually, day by day, cut the stem from the parent plant, until the plant is surviving on an independent root system. The attractive fruiting plant can then be taken to the dining table.

CARING FOR CITRUS TREES

The citrus family – oranges, lemons, kumquats and their siblings – are in flower this month. Often temperamental, they prefer a winter temperature of 5°C (41°F) at night and slightly higher during the day. They dislike sudden changes in temperature or humidity. The Victorians used charcoal around their roots, sat them on a pebble tray or misted them regularly, to ensure a humid atmosphere, and fed them once a month with a high phosphorus fertilizer.

Experts today use a free-draining compost for young plants made up of JI No. 2 with about 20% by volume of composted 'potting grade' bark. Larger plants have the same mixture but with JI No. 3. All pots and tubs should have a drainage layer of crocks at the bottom. Many members of the family are not lime tolerant and need to be watered with soft water. (See also Plants of the Month p.135.)

Citrus plants may become infested with scale insects (see p.47). One remedy is to dab the insects with a fine paint brush dipped in methylated spirits and then scratch them off with your nail.

practical project

FRUIT IN THE
CONSERVATORY
continued

FORCING STRAWBERRIES

A 'tower' of flowering and fruiting strawberries is very attractive and takes less space than the equivalent number of pots. However, forcing strawberries in ordinary pots works just as well.

YOU WILL NEED

A strawberry 'tower' (or 12 15cm (6in) pots)
JI No. 2 compost or all-purpose peat-based compost
12 strawberry plants (which can be bought from a specialist or be well-rooted runners from the garden (see p.69)
Trowel

■ For the earliest fruits, plant a cultivar like 'Pantagruella' as early as possible in the month. Water the plants well at first but moderately afterwards.

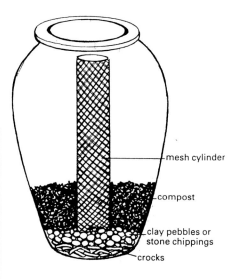

mesh cylinder

compost

clay pebbles or stone chippings

crocks

■ Keep the pots or tower out-of-doors in a sunny, sheltered position until the beginning of spring.

■ Take care that the plants are neither over-watered by winter rains nor dry out.

■ Bring them into the conservatory in late winter (having inspected them for unwelcome guests like slugs and snails first) and place the pots where there is maximum light.

■ Examine the plants for aphids, mildew and red spider mite and treat as necessary.

■ Water sparingly and ventilate the conservatory well whenever the temperature rises above 13°C (55°F).

■ Pollinate the plants by brushing the flowers daily with a soft paint brush.

■ If the leaves become pale, give a liquid feed once a week with a solution of phostrogen – 5gms (1 tsp) in 9 litres (2 gallons) of water.

■ As soon as the fruits begin to swell, increase the watering considerably and try to keep the temperature to 18°C (64°F).

RECOMMENDED VARIETIES

'Cambridge Vigour', 'Gorella', 'Elsanta', 'Hapil'
'Cambridge Late Pine

PERPETUAL FRUITING
'Aromel', 'Gento', 'Ostara', 'Rapella'

■ Perpetual fruiting cultivars such as 'Aromel' can be planted as late as spring and fruit the following autumn. Water them moderately until the fruit has set, and then more heavily. Bring the plants indoors as soon as the nights become cold.

GROWING DWARF PEACHES, NECTARINES AND APRICOTS

YOU WILL NEED

Selected variety of fruit bush
30–38cm (12–15in) tub or pot
JI No. 3 potting compost

Dwarf varieties of peaches, apricots and nectarines are widely available from garden centres. These do not need pruning. They are ideal for growing in pots and make fine flowering plants. The peach, 'Garden Silver', has rich pink flowers and white-fleshed fruit. There is also a nectarine called 'Garden Beauty' with double pink flowers. These flower early, and although they can be left out-of-doors during the winter, they may be at risk from peach leaf curl and then frosting of flowers. Bring the pots inside from early winter. You will need to hand-pollinate the plants, as with other indoor fruits. As soon as the fruits begin to form, give a high-potash liquid feed fortnightly. Thin the fruits if necessary. (See p.56.)

PLANTING PEACH, NECTARINE, APRICOT AND FIG TREES

The sunny wall of a conservatory is a perfect situation for peach, nectarine or apricot. The wall should be at least 3m (10ft) high. Peaches and nectarines need to be kept quite cool in the winter (a few degrees of frost will not harm them) but protected during blossom time and given a humid atmosphere during the growing season.

Young plants can be planted in the conservatory border and trained as fans or espaliers, or grown in 30cm (12in) pots.

■ First fix wires 30cm (12in) apart to the wall using vine eyes.

■ In the border plant the trees in good, well-drained soil. In pots use JI No. 3 with extra grit and sand.

■ Set the plants 15–20cm (6–8in) from the wall and tie the shoots in.

■ After planting prune soft unripened wood from the stem back to a plump bud.

■ You can train the trees to shape yourself (see Bibliography for suitable books) or buy them ready trained.

Figs can produce two crops each year if given indoor protection. They do well in tubs or pots as they fruit better with their roots restricted. They can be grown as bushes or half standards; bushes are cheaper to buy. All have an additional bonus of very striking leaves.

UNUSUAL FRUITING PLANTS

Apricot vine, *Passiflora incarnata*
Brazilian cherry, *Eugenia uniflora*
Fuchsia corymbiflora
Loquat, *Eriobotrya japonica*
Yellow cherry guava, *Psidium littorale lucidum*

FRUIT TREES FOR CONSERVATORIES

Apricots – 'Moorpark' and 'Alfred'
Peaches – 'Duke of York', 'Peregrine' or 'Rochester'

Nectarines – 'Lord Napier' and 'Pineapple'

Figs – The following do well indoors:
'Adam', 'Angelique', 'Fig d'Or', 'Lisa', 'Malta'
More commonly available are: 'Brown Turkey', 'Black Ischia', 'Brunshill'
These will also do well on a garden wall.

RECOMMENDED FRUITS

PEACH
'Bonanza'
'Garden Annie'
'Garden Lady'
'Terrace Amber' – yellow fruit

NECTARINE
'Nectarella'
'Terrace Ruby'

APRICOT
'Aprigold'
'Golden Glow'

plants

OF THE

month

2

CLASSIC
CONSERVATORY
PLANTS

CATEGORIES
The plants featured here are not given any category – they are simply classic conservatory plants.

OLEANDER
(*Nerium oleander*)

Oleanders make excellent tub plants for a conservatory. Given lots of sun, they cover themselves in flower and are easy to look after. Beware though, as every part of the plant is poisonous.

type	Evergreen shrub
flowers	Clusters of pink, tubular flowers with five petal-like lobes that spread out flat
leaves	Leathery, lance-shaped
height	2–3m (6–10ft)
spread	1.2–2m (4–6½ft)
temperature	2–7°C (36–45°F)
position	Sunny
planting	In border, tubs or 25–30cm (10–12in) pots
compost	JI No. 2
care	Plant in spring. Water freely during summer but withhold water and reduce flowering shoots by about half after flowering. Repot every year or two in spring. Give a weak liquid feed every two weeks in summer
propagation	Sow seeds in mid-spring at a temperature of 18–21°C (64–70°F) or take 8–10cm (3–4in) cuttings of semi-ripe shoots in early summer and root in a sandy cutting compost at 16–18°C (61–64°F). Pot the cuttings into 8cm (3in) pots of JI No. 1 and grow on in the conservatory
species and varieties	*N. oleander* 'Variegatum' has cream variegated leaves; *N. oleander* 'Géant des Batailles' has double, deep red flowers; *N. oleander* 'Luteum Plenum' has large, double yellow blooms; *N. oleander* 'Soleil Levant' is single, orange-pink. Single and double white forms are also available

CAPE LEADWORT
(*Plumbago auriculata*)

No Victorian conservatory was complete without a plumbago covering the wall and much of the roof, showing off its racemes of soft-blue flowers.

type	Evergreen climber
flowers	Trusses of primrose-shaped sky-blue flowers
leaves	Elliptical mid-green, about 8cm (3in) long
height	3m (10ft) or more
spread	1.8m (6ft) or more
temperature	4°C (39°F)
position	Good light, some sun
planting	In border, with the long arching canes trained on wires, strings or trellis
compost	JI No. 3
care	Water freely from mid-spring to mid-autumn. Thin out stems as necessary after flowering. Cutting back into old wood may be essential at times but will reduce flowering the following year
propagation	Take 8–10cm (3–4in) long heel cuttings in summer and insert three or four into 8cm (3in) pot of peat and sand. Root at a temperature of 16–18°C (61–64°F)
species and varieties	*P. auriculata* var. *alba* has white flowers

BOUGAINVILLEA
(*Bougainvillea* 'Miss Manila')

The brilliantly coloured bracts of the bougainvillea instantly recreate a sub-tropical atmosphere in the conservatory. Given the right conditions it can be persuaded to flower and produce the vivid papery bracts several times a year.

type	Evergreen climber
flowers	The flowers are small and creamy white. It is the papery bracts round them which give the plant its vivid colour. In this variety, they are a brilliant pink
leaves	Narrowly heart-shaped, green
height	To 5m (15ft)
spread	To 5m (15ft)
temperature	7°C (45°F). Below 10°C (50°F) they are deciduous
position	As sunny as possible
planting	Border or 30cm (12in) tubs or clay pots. Do not let the roots overheat in a plastic pot. Good drainage is essential
compost	JI No. 3 for mature plants
care	Plant out or repot in late winter to early spring. Shorten main stems by one-third and prune back laterals to a spur in late winter. Feed weekly with a liquid fertilizer, beginning with a high nitrogen one and changing to a high potash fertilizer like Tomorite. Keep well watered during the flowering period. Can stand outside during the summer if

PASSION FLOWER
(*Passiflora* 'Incense')

The passion flowers are known for their beautiful and intricate flowers. But beware, they can be very vigorous. *P.* 'Incense' is less tender than many of the species and not such a rampant grower.

type	Evergreen climber
flowers	10–13cm (4–5in) wide, fragrant, in shades of violet, with crowns banded in white
leaves	Palmate, with 5–7 narrow lobes
height	3–4.5m (10–15ft)
temperature	0–7°C (32–45°F)
position	Sunny
planting	Shallow border or large pot or tub (30cm (12in) in diameter). Tie shoots into trellis or plastic mesh until tendrils develop
compost	JI No. 3
care	Water freely from spring to early autumn, more sparingly in winter. In late winter or early spring, thin out the stems. Lateral shoots can be cut back
propagation	Passion flowers can be increased by layering in summer or from seed sown in mid-spring at a temperature of 21°C (70°F). Alternatively, take 8–12cm (3–4in) long sections of stem in midsummer and root in cutting compost at a temperature of 16–18°C (61–64°F). When rooted pot into 9cm (3¹/₂in) pots of JI No. 2
species and varieties	*P. caerulea* is the species most commonly seen and will grow out-of-doors in a sheltered site in warm areas. It is too vigorous for most conservatories. *P. racemosa* has crimson flowers that hang down in long racemes. It needs a warmer conservatory, with a minimum temperature of 10°C (50°F). *P. mollissima*, the banana passion flower, has pink flowers with no obvious corona filaments. It is another less rampant species

required. Some experts can achieve four flower flushes a year with a regular routine of pruning, feeding and heavy watering followed by a dry resting period. After flowering, prune and shape the plants, keeping them to about 1m (3ft) high. Remove all twiggy growth and feed with a fertilizer high in potash and trace elements

propagation Take 8cm (3in) long semi-ripe shoots in summer and root them in a sandy cutting compost in a propagator with a temperature of 21–24°C (70–75°F). Pot into JI No. 1 and then, when older, into JI No. 2 and then 3

species and varieties The species *B. glabra* has brilliant cerise bracts and will flower from an early age. It has many good hybrids, including *B.* 'Scarlet O'Hara' which has red bracts that change to pink with age, *B.* 'Lord Willingdon' (syn. 'Smartipants') which is dwarf and mauve-pink, *B.* 'Golden Glow' (syn. *B.* 'California Gold') which is a light golden-orange and the pure white *B.* 'Jennifer Fernie'. *B.* 'Mary Palmer' is very floriferous with pink and white bracts and variegated foliage

OCTOBER

*Mid-autumn is full of surprises: the weather can still seem like a
wonderful extension of summer, or truly autumnal. Whatever the days
are like, the nights will be cool. All watering should be done in the first
half of the day from now on. If the weather is unusually cold or frost
threatens, pot-grown azaleas and tender plants will be in the
conservatory protected from the elements. In an Indian summer, as
many plants as possible should be outside ripening in the sun.*

*There will still be a fair amount of watering to do as many
conservatory plants are in full bloom and winter-flowering ones are
preparing for their moment of glory. If you look carefully, you may see
the buds on acacias and correas.*

*Passion flowers, mirabilis, hoya, brugmansia, plumbago and
streptocarpus are still in flower, as is the pretty grey-leaved twining
plant, Tweedia caerulea. This has clusters of small 5-petalled flowers
of an unusual turquoise-blue, is remarkably good-tempered and never
outgrows its position. The Scarborough lily too should be in bloom.*
Cyrtanthus purpureus, *which used to be listed as* Vallota purpureus
and then as V. speciosa, *has brilliant red flowers set off by
conspicuous yellow stamens and narrow strap-like leaves.*

*There is a sense of urgency about work in the conservatory this month.
It is the last occasion for planting hardy spring-flowering bulbs and
seeds for next spring. The conservatory must be made as light,
draught-proof and dry as possible before temperatures really sink –
and they could do, with little warning at any time from now on. Plans
must be made for heating the conservatory if numbers of large, tender
plants are to be grown and housed there. If you hope to bring in some
herbaceous plants from the garden now is the time to do that too.*

CHECKLIST ✓

▢ Plan for winter warmth
▢ Bring the garden indoors
▢ Watch for pests

tasks

FOR THE

month

ROUTINE TASKS

Remove all shading and blinds. Use the maximum and minimum thermometer to discover the conservatory's micro-climates. Move tender plants to the warmest part of the conservatory at night. If frost is forecast, cover plants with a layer of newspaper or horticultural fleece

Many plants will need to be watered sparingly from now on

Clivias and *Cyrtanthus purpureus* should not be dried off absolutely during the winter. Now is a good time for buying and potting these bulbs. Use good compost and a pot that just holds the bulb comfortably. Both like to be pot-bound like the one shown below

● PLANNING FOR WINTER WARMTH

The ideal conservatory has double glazing, thermostatically controlled heating, automatic ventilation plus a water supply and a tiled floor with a drain in it. Most of us have to make do with conditions that are far from perfect. If we selected our plants with care we would have no problems. However, being human and being gardeners, we all lack perfect self-discipline. Come mid-autumn, most conservatory owners suddenly realise that during the warm months of summer they have been seduced by glamorous orchids, exotic passion flowers and tender tibouchinas. Unlike fuchsias and pelargoniums they cannot be allowed to dry out or be stored under the spare bed!

All those irresistible plants from the tropics, with magnificent flowers and heart-stopping scents, are going to need some special treatment to get them through the winter. If plans have not already been made, now is the time to think about heating if there are any plants that need a higher minimum temperature than 5°C (41°F).

A conservatory facing full sun, built against a house wall, sheltered from the coldest winds and with solid brick lower walls, will not get as cold as a greenhouse. For sudden cold snaps, opening a door into the house should keep the temperature above freezing. An electric fan heater set to 6°C (43°F) when several degrees of frost are forecast is not too expensive as it may only need to be used on a few nights each year. (See also p.12.)

If the conservatory is more shady, more exposed or contains several large trees and shrubs that need a much higher temperature to survive, it is a good idea to run a radiator off the central heating system. It will need a separate thermostat and control, because it has to go on at night and probably switch off during the day. Paraffin heaters are cheap to buy and to run, but need to be kept scrupulously clean. They also increase the moisture in the air.

A few small, very tender plants can be protected in a thermostatically controlled electric propagator with a high lid. The sand bench (see Practical Project p.136) with a frame over which horticultural fleece and bubble polythene can be fixed, will take more and taller plants. A double-walled outdoor cloche over the warmed sand is very effective. None of these are particularly attractive for the

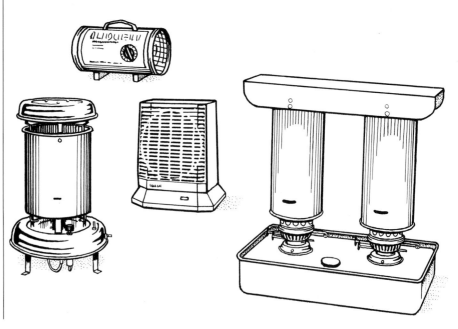

ideal 'drawing room with plants' but they can be sited so they are not in full view from the living rooms of the house, or they can be camouflaged a little with hardier plants.

The same blinds that shade the conservatory in summer can be very useful for insulation in winter, particularly at night. If more permanent forms of insulation are planned, such as fitting sheets of bubble polythene (which is generally agreed to be the most effective of the plastic sheets), it is important to clean the glass well before fixing it on. In the north of Britain, insulation will need installing now. Further south, do not be in too much of a hurry to insulate or to heat the conservatory — many plants need some form of winter rest. Keeping the plants dry will enable many of them to adjust to lower temperatures. The cells are not plumped up with sap and so there is space for expansion if temperatures drop to below the usual minimum suggested for the plant. But — be prepared.

BRINGING THE GARDEN INDOORS

Garden plants can make their own contribution to a colourful display in the conservatory. Spring-flowering perennials such as *Dicentra spectabilis*, hellebores, astilbes, polyanthus and *Primula denticulata* can be carefully dug out of the ground, with as much root as possible, and potted up in good potting compost into the smallest pot that they will fit in. Keep them in a cold frame or keep the pots plunged in ashes or sand (to prevent the roots from freezing solid in the pots) and bring them into the conservatory when required from midwinter onwards. In a cold conservatory, they will flower earlier than they would

in the garden. If there is heat they will flower very rapidly.

Half-hardy bedding plants like petunias and busy lizzies can be given a new lease of life. Dig a few plants up from the garden borders before the first frosts and pot them up in good compost. Cut the plants hard back and they should flower again during the winter. Many of the tender bedding plants that are treated as annuals in this country are in fact perennials in their native lands, and provided with the right amount of heat, will behave as they do at home.

PEST WATCH

As soon as the temperature begins to fall, pests seem less of a problem. Unfortunately, they do not go away completely, but begin to hibernate. Then they will emerge next spring with voracious appetites. Good hygiene now will reduce the numbers that overwinter in a cosy conservatory (see April Tasks).

■ *Red spider mites* These become brick-red and look for dark crevices in the structure of the building itself and in the soil. Infected plants should be destroyed.

■ *Aphids* Give a last spray against greenfly and discard heavily infested plants.

■ *Scale insects* In a warm conservatory, these breed all year. In cooler conditions they reproduce only in spring and summer but they overwinter on dormant plants. They can sometimes be removed by wiping the stems with a damp cloth. Fruit trees, including grape vines, can be given a tar oil winter wash. Badly infested shoots should be pruned out and destroyed. Malathion or pirimiphos-methyl sprays can be used all

year in the conservatory. They are most effective against the nymphs or young scale insect.

■ *Whiteflies* do not hibernate and yellow sticky traps are a good control and equally as effective during the winter. Shake or brush the plants so that the whitefly rise up and get caught on the traps. Carefully inspect beneath the underside of the leaves of affected plants. Whitefly nymphs look a little like tiny aphids and can be squashed — but do not damage the leaf while doing this. Clear away any weeds from around the conservatory as these can provide places for whitefly to overwinter. Old woody plants could be replaced with new, uninfested, cuttings.

■ *Leafminers* are a particular problem with cinerarias and chrysanthemums. Remove all dead leaves from the soil and any plants of the daisy family that might provide hibernating places for this pest.

There are other larger pests which may invade the conservatory in the autumn. Watch out for them.

■ *Slugs* are very active at this time. If there are any of the characteristic slimy trails in and around the conservatory, scatter a very few slug pellets in the area.

■ *Mice* like to move indoors for the winter. Check that there are no holes for them to use. Seal any doubtful places near ground level. Bait and traps are effective.

■ *Woodlice* hibernate in cracks and in piles of pots and seed trays. Check these and store them somewhere else if possible. Brickwork may need repointing and gaps around window frames, sealed. Dust likely hiding places with HCH dust.

ROUTINE TASKS

The tubers of begonias, gloxinias (sinningias) and achimenes should be dried off during this month. Shake the soil from begonia tubers and store in dry coconut fibre; leave the sinningias in their compost. Both should be stored in a dry, frostproof but cool place

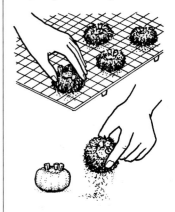

Sow seed of parsley for use at Christmas

Sow seeds of *Linaria maroccana*, *L. reticulata* 'Crown Jewels' and *Salpiglossis sinuata* 'Casino mixed' for spring flowers (see p.98)

Continue to plant spring-flowering bulbs like tulips and muscari this month to provide a succession of flowers in the spring

Keep potted azaleas well-watered — they will be coming into flower in the next two months

Shoots of climbers can be thinned out to allow more light in

Any prepared bulbs of narcissi or hyacinth that were planted in late summer should be brought from plunge beds into the conservatory if the shoots are about 2.5cm (1in) high and buds are showing

Keep the conservatory well ventilated day and night if it contains vines, peaches or chrysanthemums. These particular fruits and flowers do not make ideal companions for tender plants because they need cool autumn and winter conditions and good ventilation

plants
OF THE
month
1

 KASHMIR CYPRESS

(Cupressus torulosa 'Cashmeriana'*)*

This conifer has pendent branchlets from which the blue-green leaves hang, creating a graceful waterfall effect. In the wild the Kashmir cypress can reach 18m (60ft), but when grown in a pot, it remains much smaller while retaining its pyramidal shape and its elegance.

category	Easy
type	Evergreen tree
flowers	A mature specimen will have small, greenish-yellow cones
leaves	Flat, glaucous-blue sprays
height	1.8m (6ft)
spread	1m (3ft)
temperature	7°C (45°F)
position	Good light
planting	Unless the conservatory is very large, restrain in a pot or tub
compost	JI No. 3

care	Repot in early spring every other year. Prune gently, then, if absolutely necessary, but do not cut hard back as this will spoil the shape. Ventilate well if the temperature rises above 27°C (80°F)
propagation	Difficult! Take 10cm (4in) heel shoots in summer and insert in cutting compost in a propagator. Some bottom heat is needed and nothing may happen for a year

 NERINE

(Nerine bowdenii)

In some parts *N. bowdenii* will grow happily out-of-doors at the foot of a sunny wall. It is the hardiest member of its family and frequently grown for its showy umbels of bright-pink twisted flowers.

category	Easy
type	Bulb
flowers	Heads of five to ten pink flowers with wavy margined, recurved petals
leaves	Upright, strap-shaped
height	46–60cm (18–24in)
spread	13–15cm (5–6in)
temperature	4°C (39°F)
position	Full sun
planting	Three bulbs to a 13–15cm (5–6in) pot with good drainage layer or 10cm (4in) deep in sunny well-drained border
compost	JI No. 2 with extra sand
care	Keep cool and dry from autumn to spring. When the leaves appear, begin to water and water freely until leaves begin to turn yellow. Then withhold water and dry the

plants off again. Repot every four or five years in late summer. Nerines dislike disturbance

propagation Separate and pot up offsets when the plant is being repotted. Use the same compost and care

species and N. bowdenii 'Pink Triumph' is deep
varieties pink; N. undulata is palest pink with crinkled flowers and is only 30cm (12in) high. N. sarniensis, the Guernsey lily, has salmon-red flowers and needs a minimum temperature of 10°C (50°F). N. filifolia is smaller, with narrow leaves and rose-red flowers, 2.5cm (1in) long

PERSIAN VIOLET
(*Exacum affine*)

E. affine is a compact cushion-shaped annual, studded with cheerful, fragrant flowers which last for a long period. It is easy to grow from seed (although it can be bought as a pot plant) and is undemanding.

category Fragrant
type Annual
flowers Shallow bowl-shaped, purple flowers, 1–2cm ($^1/_2$–$^3/_4$in) across with bright yellow stamens. Fragrant
leaves Oval, mid-green
height 23–30m (9–12in)
spread 23–30m (9–12in)
temperature 13–16°C (55–61°F)
position Good light but shade during hottest months
planting 13cm (5in) pots
compost JI No. 2
care Ensure good ventilation when the temperature rises above 16°C (61°F). Keep well-watered and give a liquid feed every fortnight from midsummer to early autumn
propagation Sow the seeds thinly on the top of a tray of lightly firmed seed compost in autumn for the best plants, or in early spring. Maintain a temperature of 18°C (64°F). Cover the trays with glass or polythene. Water from below. When the seedlings are large enough to handle, prick them out into small pots and when the roots fill these, pot on into the final containers
species and White and lavender-pink varieties
varieties may be available

ASPIDISTRA
(*Aspidistra elatior*)

The aspidistra was called the cast-iron plant by the Victorians because it could survive almost any conditions. It is a handsome foliage plant and makes a good foil for brighter flowering plants.

category Cool and shady
type Evergreen perennial
flowers Only rarely produces cream to purple tiny flowers on short stalks
leaves Long, 60cm (24in), narrow, dark green
height 60cm (2ft)
spread 46cm (18in)
temperature 7–10°C (45–50°F)
position Shade
planting 15cm (6in) pot in early spring
compost JI No. 2
care Water well in summer and sparingly in winter, keeping the soil just moist. Repot every two or three years in early spring if necessary, although the aspidistra really enjoys being pot-bound. Keep potting on up to a 25cm (10in) pot if very large plant wanted. Give a weak liquid feed every four weeks in summer
propagation Divide and replant the roots in spring
species and A. elatior 'Variegata' has cream-
varieties striped leaves

practical project 1

PAINTING TERRACOTTA POTS

A group of distinctive containers can make an attractive feature in a conservatory, even without a single plant. For the non-gardener this might be the ultimate solution! Adding some of the easier evergreen plants to the containers, however, can enhance the characteristics of the conservatory and create an indoor garden with very little trouble. Elaborate pots need simple plants, while showy plants look better in plainer containers.

Terracotta has many qualities that make it ideal for containing plants. The bright colour of new terracotta pots, however, does not always blend comfortably with the flowers in it. Painting the pots is one way of ensuring that the colours of pot and flower always complement each other. If you are gifted with the paintbrush you can give full rein to your creativity, and produce a stunning and unique collection of containers like those shown in the illustration. However, some of us may find our talents somewhat more limited so the simple method of decoration described in this project is designed to come within the realm of the less artistically inclined

Several containers of different sizes and shapes can be visually linked by treating the painting of them all in the same way.

●
METHOD

■ Dilute about two-thirds of the acrylic paint with a teacupful of water.

■ Then add some of the Polyfilla to make a paste. Add the Polyfilla slowly until you get the right thickness for painting on to the pot.

■ Do not add too much water or Polyfilla at once or you may find that the mixture has become

too pale and you run out of paint to colour it with!

■ Apply the tinted paste with the brush. The paste will lighten in colour as it dries. If it does not seem dark enough as you are mixing it, add some more diluted paint.

■ Create a textured appearance by quickly brushing over the pot with neat acrylic paint before the first layer has dried.

■ You will probably need some practice with this to get a natural effect so begin with a small pot.

■ To give a gleam to the Polyfilla, which can look rather chalky, smooth over the painted surface with a rag soaked in French polish. This has a yellowish tinge and alters the colour of the finished pot.

YOU WILL NEED

Terracotta pots
0.5kg pack of exterior Polyfilla
Tube of acrylic paint
Different acrylic colours can be mixed to get the exact shade required, but use just one of them as the texturing top coat
Bottle of French polish
Bowl (to mix the filler and paint in)
An old spoon
Paint brush 2.5cm (1in) wide (or wider, if the pot is very large)

EASY EVERGREENS FOR PAINTED POTS

Aspidistra elatior
Bay (Laurus nobilis)
Chaemerops humilis
Cheeseplant (Monstera deliciosa)
Cupressus torulosa 'Cashmeriana'
Fatsia japonica
Ficus elastica
Nephrolepis exaltata and cvs
Phoenix roebelinii
Pittosporum tobira
Schleffera actinophylla

plants
OF THE
month
2

A collection of orchids provides such an exotic display of colour in the conservatory that it is well worth taking the trouble required to cultivate them. Cymbidiums (centre) are the easiest orchids to grow in the conservatory. Phalaenopsis (bottom right) are better as house plants. Other genera shown here include × Brassocattleya, Miltoniopsis, Paphiopedilum, Lemboglossum, Rossioglossum and Zygopetalum, which require more specialized treatment

ORCHIDS
(Cymbidium hybrids*)*

Orchids are among the most desirable and beautiful of flowering plants. The orchid family contains 20,000 species and many thousands more hybrids. They are expensive to buy and fussy about their conditions. Cymbidiums are among the easiest to grow and the miniature hybrids are irresistible. Flower colours range from white to dark red, with many combinations of veining and shading and each flower spike will last for two to three months.

category	Challenging
type	Evergreen terrestrial orchid
flowers	Spikes of from six to twenty blooms which consist of five flat petals and sepals at the top and a 3-lobed lip, often spotted or differently coloured at the bottom
leaves	Long and narrow, emerging from 'pseudobulbs'
height	30–60cm (12–24in)
spread	25cm (10in)
temperature	Night: 11.5–14°C (53–57°F); day: 16–20°C (61–68°F)
position	Good light essential. Stand outside in summer in a semi-shaded position to start with, and then move gradually to a sunnier position. This is to harden the plant to the increased light out-of-doors and to initiate the flower spikes for the next season. Acclimatize it in a similar way when bringing the plant indoors in early autumn
planting	Choose a pot that is slightly larger than the plant, to allow for one or two years' growth only. The pseudobulbs should be placed at the back of the pot with the base of the pseudobulbs at the surface of the compost. New growth occurs at the front of the plant
compost	Either a mixture of 2 parts fibrous peat, with ground chalk and dolomite added to bring up to a pH of 6.2, and 1 part of coarse Perlite; or absorbent rockwool. Most orchid nurseries sell special orchid compost or rockwool
care	Never allow the compost to become waterlogged and stagnant. Stand the pot on a tray of moist gravel to increase humidity but do *not* let the pot sit in water. Pick any remaining flowers by the end of late spring. As the temperature increases, feed regularly with special orchid fertilizer but every fourth watering, omit the fertilizer so that any excess salts are washed out of the compost. The orchid should make new shoots. Stand outside from the middle of summer. Do not give any fertilizer during the first month that the orchid is standing outside. Bring indoors again before the first frosts. Repot in spring or directly after flowering. When the orchid is too large for the pot and has several leafless pseudobulbs, it can be divided. Make sure that each section has three healthy pseudobulbs and then follow the instructions for planting
propagation	By division when repotting (see above). Old leafless back bulbs, provided they are not shrivelled, can also be used for propagation. Plant them individually in 8cm (3in) pots in orchid compost, positioning the cut side of the bulb nearest the pot. Put the pot in a cool, shady place and keep it moist. If you are lucky, in two or three months a healthy new shoot should appear
species and varieties	There are many cymbidium hybrids in a wide range of colours. Modern hybrids have been bred for vigour and ease of cultivation and are an ideal choice for a beginner. *C.* Showgirl 'Anna' is a miniature with subtle greenish flowers and dark red markings. Other orchids that are suitable for conservatories are the almost hardy pleiones and bletillas which only need to be kept frost free. The beautiful moth orchids, the phalaenopsis species and hybrids, need higher temperatures, above 16.5°C (62°F) at night and up to 30°C (85°F) during the day, without direct sunlight. They are better as pot plants in a centrally heated house

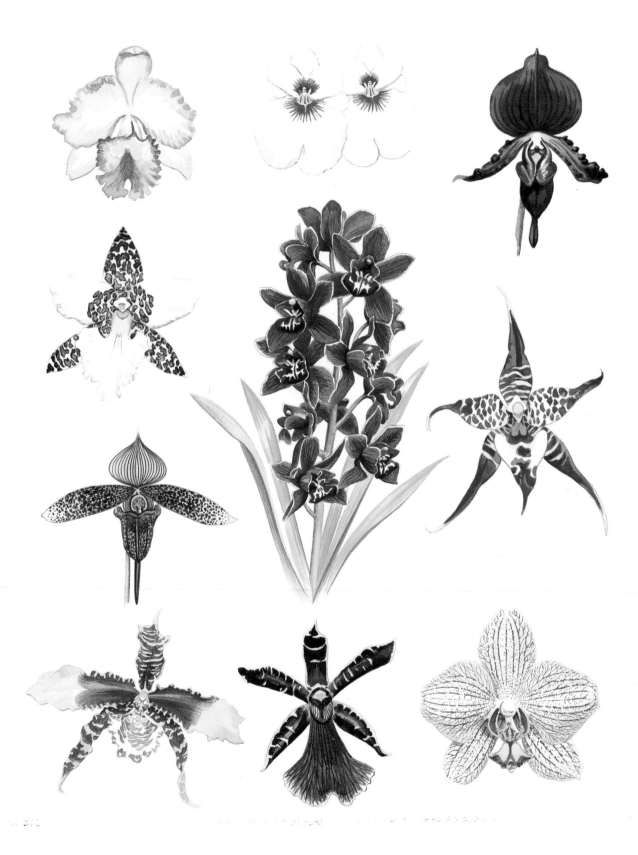

practical project 2

MAKING A PLANTING BOX

NOTE
Imperial measurements given are not exact conversions but are the equivalents as used by most hardware stores selling wood.

PLANTS FOR A PLANTING BOX

Bamboo
Buddleia asiatica
Camellia cvs
Daphne odora **'Aureomarginata'**
Hydrangeas
Fuchsias, trailing and upright
Hibiscus
Ivy *(Hedera)* spp.

Grouping different plants in one container is also very effective. Hanging baskets, window boxes and patio tubs look as well in the conservatory as they do outside. An elegant planting box that will hold a selection of different plants at different times of the year is easy to construct.

YOU WILL NEED

Drill, Saw, Screws
Nails, Hammer, Spirit level
Wood glue, Screwdriver
Sandpaper (coarse, medium and fine)
Oil-based paint for undercoat and topcoat

- *5.5mm (¹/₄in) exterior-grade plywood (or Wainscot boards) 60 x 135cm (24 x 53in)*
- *(a) Four 35cm (14in) lengths of 46 x 46mm (1³/₄ x 1³/₄in) softwood*
- *(b) Four 30cm (12in) lengths of 46 x 19mm (1³/₄ x ³/₄in) softwood*
- *(c) Four 60cm (24in) lengths of 46 x 19mm (1³/₄ x ³/₄in) softwood*
- *(d) Eight 30cm (12in) strips of 21 x 21mm (⁷/₈ x ⁷/₈in) batten*
- *(e) Two 30cm (12in) lengths of 21 x 21mm (⁷/₈ x ⁷/₈in) batten*
- *(f) Two 55cm (22in) lengths of 21 x 21mm (⁷/₈ x ⁷/₈in) batten*
- *Four decorative finials (or wooden door knobs)*

CONSTRUCTION

- Glue and screw battens (d) on to the adjoining faces of the 46 x 46mm (1³/₄ x 1³/₄in) uprights (a), 2.5cm (1in) from the top and the bottom and flush with the edges.

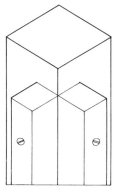

- Cut four panels from the plywood: two end panels 35 x 30cm (14 x 12in) and the two facing panels 35 x 60cm (14 x 24in). Glue and screw these panels to the outer cross pieces (b) and (c). Use small screws and work from the back.

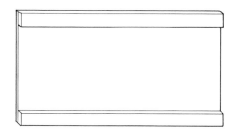

- Cut the base panel 30 x 60cm (12 x 24in) and saw a 25 x 25mm (1 x 1in) square from each corner.

- Fix rails of 21 x 21mm (⁷/₈ x ⁷/₈in) along all sides inside the box, for the base panel or a sturdy plastic tray to rest on. Glue and pin these battens (e) and (f) to the inside of the plywood panels.

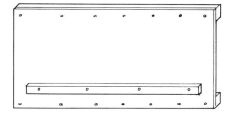

- Attach each panel to the strips (d) that have been joined to the uprights (a), with wood glue and screws. Join the four sides together to make the complete rectangle.

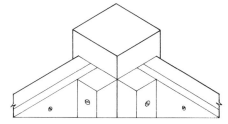

● FINISHING

■ When the planter has been assembled, sand it well. Apply two undercoats and one top coat of paint. Paint the finials at the same time. The panels can be painted to resemble wood strips or trellis (see panel).

■ Finally, screw in the finials.

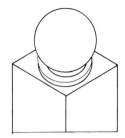

A finished corner post with finial

NOVEMBER

The days are short, and mists, fogs, and damp, rotting leaves are features of the garden outside. In the conservatory, however, winter has been arrested. Unless there has been a prolonged cold spell, a gratifying number of the loveliest plants may still be in flower: Pandorea, Lapageria, Cassia corymbosa, Bougainvillea, Jasminum sambac, Citrus and passion flower. Foliage, that in the garden has been damaged by wind, frost and rain, is still fresh and unspoiled inside. The brilliant leaves of the variegated abutilon look as if the sun is out all year. The first cinerarias, cyclamen, Begonia 'Gloire de Lorraine', Primula kewensis and P. obconica are coming into bloom. Already there are noticeable flower buds on the camellias – forecasting spring before the onset of winter.

Yet this is a difficult time in the conservatory: there is need for constant vigilance, but not much essential activity. On bright days it is still warm enough to sit in if there is space left among the azaleas, camellias, potted-up shrubs, bulbs planted for forcing and the tender plants from the terrace and patio that have been moved indoors to protect them from the weather and to extend their flowering season. There are still dramatic fluctuations in temperature: a sudden frost at night makes the temperature in the conservatory drop surprisingly low and on a bright day the thermometer can rise steeply, causing wilt in plants that are being kept on the dry side for the winter. Feeding should be kept to a minimum and restricted to plants in flower. Only pot-bound plants need repotting.

Make time this month for rearranging the conservatory. Have fun grouping foliage plants, moving forward some of the plants that will soon be in flower and hiding those that are past their best. The climbers that have outgrown their places during the summer can be cut back, tidied up, any dead leaves removed and long stems tied in. Creating a new stage set for the winter show can be extremely satisfying.

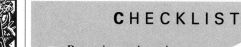

tasks

FOR THE

month

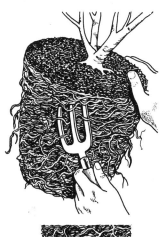

REPOTTING AND POTTING ON

Although this is not the best time of the year to repot, it may be necessary if, when you bring plants indoors from the garden, you notice that they have become pot-bound. Seedlings may have become too large for their pots. Unless the plant seems to be actively growing and flowering, use a JI No. 1 compost which will

hold sufficient moisture for it, yet will not stimulate plants into growth at the wrong time of year by providing food.

Cuttings of tender plants, such as fuchsias and pelargoniums, that ʰave rooted since they were taken in late summer, will also need potting on this month. Pot them up into 8cm (3in) pots using JI No. 2 compost. For pelargoniums, mix extra sand and grit in with the compost because they need sharp drainage.

Hardy annuals sown for early spring-flowering may also need potting on again. They should never be allowed to become pot-bound as this causes premature flowering. Use JI No. 1 or 2 and, at this time of year, move them only from a 7–9cm (3–3¹⁄₂in) pot to a 10cm (4in) pot. The pots should not be placed too close to each other as this restricts air circulation.

Botrytis or grey mould may be a problem and can be prevented by ensuring a dry atmosphere and good ventilation. On cold, misty days, open the door between the house and the conservatory for several hours. If the conservatory opens off the kitchen where steam is likely to be present from cooking or washing, then keep the door closed and well sealed, particularly in the evening. The combination of moist warm air on the cold glass of the conservatory will be detrimental to both the plants and the fabric of the conservatory.

Composts

Loam- or soil-based composts are recommended for conservatory plants. From now on, plants in the conservatory need to be kept fairly dry, but not dried out. This is easier to control in a soil-based compost, which does not dry out as quickly as those with a peat base. Coconut fibre-based composts can appear to be quite dry but may actually be waterlogged at the bottom.

With a soil-based compost it is important not to form a hard surface on the top by too heavy watering. This crust throws the water off rather than absorbs it, as does over-dry peat. Use a medium rose on your watering can or make sure that the surface of the soil is broken up and can absorb the water efficiently.

For moisture-loving plants, a mixture of equal quantities of a proprietary all-purpose peat-based compost with JI No. 2 works well. Covering the pots with a thick layer of gravel or chippings helps prevent drying out.

PLANTING BULBS

It is still not too late to plant tulips, *Iris reticulata*, some narcissus and lily-of-the-valley. The latter can be dug up from the garden and potted up in any good compost, to flower inside in mid-spring. If bulbs planted in pots and left outside earlier in the year show shoots of 2.5cm (about 1in), bring them indoors. They will flower earlier. Prepared hyacinths and narcissus that were planted in early autumn can be brought into the

daylight now *if* the flower buds are emerging and showing some colour. Narcissus for late winter flowering can be planted around the middle of this month and put in a cold, dark place for 6–10 weeks.

PRUNING PEACHES AND NECTARINES

Fan training fruit trees ensures that they do not take over the conservatory and that the fruits receive the maximum amount of sun. Peaches form their blossom buds on shoots produced during the previous season.

PRUNING PEACHES

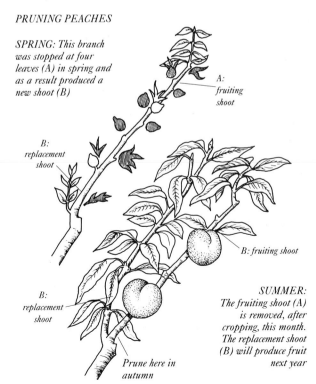

SPRING: This branch was stopped at four leaves (A) in spring and as a result produced a new shoot (B)

A: fruiting shoot

B: replacement shoot

B: fruiting shoot

B: replacement shoot

Prune here in autumn

SUMMER: The fruiting shoot (A) is removed, after cropping, this month. The replacement shoot (B) will produce fruit next year

Winter pruning of fan-trained trees consists of cutting each parent shoot, that fruited this year, back to the basal shoot, which will make the replacement growth. Tie them in on the supporting wires. The replacement shoots need to radiate evenly, about 8cm (3in) apart. The wall behind the tree may need re-painting. Now is a good time to do it. Then give the tree a tar oil winter wash.

PRUNING TENDER PLANTS

Plumbago, oleander, hibiscus, passion flowers and daturas (now *Brugmansia*) can be pruned this month. *Plumbago auriculata* may need tidying up, by removing some stems completely and cutting back others. It is a very vigorous plant if growing in a border, and can exclude light from the conservatory if not kept in check. Use sharp secateurs or a knife and always cut just

above a node. *Nerium oleander* can have all stems cut back by half after flowering. *Brugmansia* will also need cutting back after flowering. If you want to be drastic, all these three will tolerate being cut hard back if it is necessary.

GROWING FRESH HERBS

Roots or clumps of chives, parsley, French tarragon and any of the mints can be lifted from the garden, divided and potted-up in a good soil-based compost to provide supplies of fresh green leaves over the winter. Water the pots well and cut back the old top growth. New shoots will soon appear. The pots need to be kept in a light place in the conservatory, out of draughts.

THINKING AHEAD

Although not all seed firms have a wide range of conservatory plants, most supply seeds for hardy and half-hardy annuals, and tender plants commonly used for bedding. Send off for catalogues and use a quiet period to plan for next year.

Be adventurous, try something new. The cupheas, or cigar plants, are evergreen and have tubular red flowers, with black rims, edged with white; *Mina lobata* is a slender annual climber that has flowers which open a crimson-red and fade through orange and yellow to white; kalanchoes are excellent winter-flowering pot plants, with large succulent leaves and vivid flowers of yellow, rose-pink and scarlet. Seeds sown in late winter will flower the following winter. *Incarvillea sinensis* 'Cheron' is about 30cm (12in) tall, has creamy-white gloxinia-like blooms, ferny foliage and flowers in ten weeks from a mid-spring sowing.

ROUTINE TASKS

Check the temperature inside and out by night and by day. If you have not done so already, bring in pots of fuchsias, pelargoniums, osteospermum and agapanthus from outside. Wrap tenderest plants in fleece or move them away from the glass

Ventilate on bright days

Water plants sparingly, in the morning if possible

Bring in herbs, late summer-sown annuals and bulbs in pots

Examine the pots carefully for snails and woodlice. Remove them or any dead leaves and other debris

plants
OF THE
month
1

ABUTILON
(Abutilon megapotamicum)

A good wall shrub for the beginner's conservatory, this abutilon has a graceful habit with long arching branches, fascinating small flowers like Christmas-tree lanterns for a large part of the year and withstands low temperatures.

category	Easy
type	Evergreen wall shrub
flowers	Hanging rich red calyces, yellow petals and a mass of protruding black stamens
leaves	Slender, pointed oval, mid-green
height	3m (10ft)
spread	3m (10ft)
temperature	3°C (37°F)
position	Sunny
planting	Border or 20–25cm (8–10in) pots
compost	JI No. 2
care	Will need supporting, either against wall or on canes. Water well during the growing season. Liquid feed every fortnight from late spring to early autumn. Pot on annually in spring. Prune back main stems by half and side shoots to 8–10cm (3–4in) at the same time, if necessary. Ventilate well when temperature exceeds 13°C (55°F)
propagation	Take cuttings of semi-ripe side shoots between late spring and late summer and insert in a cutting compost. Place pots in a propagator with a temperature of 15–18°C (59–64°F) in early to mid-spring in seed compost at a temperature of 15–18°C (59–64°F). When large enough to handle, prick out into 9cm (3½in) pots of JI No. 1. Alternatively sow seed. New plants from seed can be raised each year if required
species and varieties	There are many excellent hybrid abutilons, some with variegated leaves. They require higher temperatures than *A. megapotamicum* and do not produce their larger flowers for as long. *A.* 'Canary Bird' is yellow; *A.* 'Ashford Red' has crimson flowers, while those of *A.* 'Kentish Belle' are warm yellow and copper

CYCLAMEN
(Cyclamen persicum)

The first of the large-flowered hybrid cyclamen come into flower this month. With their white or pink flowers (named hybrids can be red or purple as well) and beautifully marked leaves they make a fine display in a cool conservatory

category	Cool and shady
type	Tuberous perennial
flowers	Slender fragrant flowers with five swept back and slightly twisted petals
leaves	Heart-shaped, dark green and marked with silver and lighter green
height	10–20cm (4–8in)
spread	15–20cm (6–8in)
temperature	5–7°C (41–45°F)
position	Good light but no direct sun
planting	Plant corm in late summer in good compost in 13cm (5in) pot
compost	JI No. 2 with added peat and leafmould
care	Water cyclamen from below to avoid getting water on the corms. Allow plenty of room between pots for plants to grow to their full size. Increase humidity by standing plant on a tray of damp gravel. Allow plant to dry off during the summer by putting the pot on its side in a shady place out-of-doors. When it begins to grow again the following summer, repot and water carefully
propagation	Sow seed in late summer or early autumn to flower fifteen months later. Sow the seeds 2.5cm (1in) apart in JI seed compost. They can be germinated outside in a shaded cold frame. Prick off the seedlings into JI No. 1 in 6cm (2½in) pots when the second leaves develop and grow on at a temperature of 16°C (61°F)
species and varieties	*C. persicum* 'Cardinal' has reddish-pink flowers; *C. persicum* 'Renown' has scarlet flowers while *C. persicum* 'Pearl Wave' has deep-pink petals with frilled edges

TEMPLE BELLS
(Smithiantha 'Orange King'*)*

A compact bushy plant with vivid flowers on slender stems held above the foliage from summer to late autumn. The beautifully marked large leaves with their rich texture make *S.* 'Orange King', and all the other *Smithiantha* hybrids, attractive for a long season.

category	Challenging
type	Rhizomatous perennial
flowers	Tubular orange-scarlet flowers, with yellow lips spotted with red

leaves	Round velvety leaves with scalloped edges, deep green marked with brown veins
height	60cm (24in)
spread	60cm (24in)
temperature	18–21°C (64–70°F) while in flower. Store rhizomes at 10–12°C (50–54°F) minimum
position	Good light but not full sun
planting	Plant each rhizome in early summer, in moist peat, in a 10–13cm (4–5in) pot. Pot on as necessary
compost	JI No. 2 or all-purpose peat-based compost
care	Water well and feed weekly from late summer onwards. Plants may need supporting with thin canes. Allow to dry off after flowering
propagation	Divide rhizomes into 5cm (2in) pieces any time between late winter and late spring. Make sure each has a strong shoot. Pot up as above
species and varieties	S. 'Pink Lady', S. 'New Yellow Hybrid' and many other hybrids in shades of red, orange and yellow

CAROLINA JASMINE ▼
(Gelsemium sempervirens)

The Carolina or False Jasmine has twining dark stems and attractive shiny, deep green leaves all year. When grown indoors it is covered with golden-yellow flowers in late autumn. The scent has been described as slightly rose-like and intensely heady. Take care though, as every part of the plant is poisonous.

category	Fragrant
type	Evergreen climber
flowers	Funnel-shaped, deep yellow flowers with darker, orange-yellow throats
leaves	Narrowly oval, pointed, glossy
height	3m (10ft)
temperature	Half-hardy, but allow temperature to fall to 5–10°C (41–50°F) in early autumn for flowers in late autumn
position	As sunny as possible
planting	As every part of the plant is poisonous, plant four cuttings in a 20cm (8in) hanging pot or basket, out of reach, in midsummer. When the stems grow, wind them round a wire frame or other support
compost	JI No. 2
care	Keep well-watered, especially when forming flower buds. Feed plant liberally in summer. Do not feed while in flower
propagation	Take semi-ripe cuttings in summer and root them in a propagator or cover the pot with a polythene bag supported on small canes and secured with an elastic band
species and varieties	G. sempervirens 'Flore Pleno' has double flowers

Temple bells

practical
project

A WINTER HERB
GARDEN

The period when fresh herbs are available can be extended by growing them in pots or other containers in the conservatory. It is also possible to grow more unusual varieties and species of aromatic herbs that need winter protection. The two groups need different conditions but both should be put outside during the summer.

YOU WILL NEED

Herb roots and plants
Parsley seed, Parsley pot
Herb pot, Large tubs
JI No. 2 potting compost
Sand, Grit
Secateurs, Trowel

CONTAINERS

Select your containers. Most herbs flourish in terracotta pots. Rosemary, myrtle and bay will need 30cm (12in) pots. Smaller herbs can be planted in specially made herb pots or parsley pots or in ordinary pots.

There are also many interesting arrangements of containers for herbs available, as well as glazed pots, wooden and fibreglass tubs. Some of the nicest arrangements of herbs that I have seen have been growing in painted tins outside houses in Mediterranean villages. Old cans of all sizes have holes punched in them and are given a lick of paint.

SUITABLE HERBS

Mint
This is one of the simplest herbs to propagate as it makes runners which root at the nodes. Separate a rooted node, plus its shoot and pot it up in good compost. If you use a lot of mint, dig up a small plant and pot it up in a 13cm (5in) pot. Cut back all the stems. Mint needs more moisture than many of the other herbs and will stand some shade.

Marjoram and thyme
Plants can be lifted from the garden and potted up. Clip back the top growth. They need good light, good ventilation and cool conditions. Plants that have been cut back and forced can be discarded or should be given a year to recover and planted out in the garden.

Basil, chervil, parsley and coriander
Seed can be sown fresh. Bear in mind there has to be a balance between light, day length and heat for annuals such as these to thrive. Heat on its own produces weak plants.

Rosemary and young sage bushes
Both will live happily in pots. Some of the more tender of these would be ideal dual-purpose conservatory plants. Two of the coloured-leaved sages, which often succumb to the vagaries of the weather outside, are very attractive while still being useful for the kitchen or medicinal purposes. *Salvia officinalis* 'Icterina' has green and gold leaves while *S. o.* 'Purpurascens Variegata' has leaves splashed with purple and cream. *Rosmarinus officinalis* is fairly hardy, but *R. angustissimus*

'Corsican Blue' and *R. a.* 'Benenden Blue', both with bright blue flowers, are tender. 'Benenden Blue' has a more trailing habit. Gold or silver striped varieties of rosemary exist and they too are tender. If the plants grow too large, root pruning is the answer.

Aromatic herbs

Grown for the pleasure of their scented leaves, include other varieties of sage, like *Salvia elegans* 'Scarlet Pineapple', myrtle, (*Myrtus communis* or the smaller *M. c. tarentina* or the variegated *M. c. t.* 'Microphylla Variegata'), lemon verbena, (*Aloysia triphylla*) the woolly lavender, *Lavendula multifida* and Balm of Gilead (*Cedronella canariensis*).

Bay trees

These are traditional conservatory plants. In the south of the country and in mild areas in the west, the bay will flourish out-of-doors, but it is still convenient to have a supply of fresh leaves close at hand during the winter. The patient gardener can buy a small plant and train it to a standard form. (See p.72.)

Ginger

You can grow ginger in a pot too. The ginger root on sale in this country is actually a rhizome. Most shops allow you to select your own piece from a container. Next time you buy a piece, look for a section of root with small greenish bumps which could be possible buds. This should produce roots and shoots if potted up and kept moist and warm. Move the growing plant to a light place out of direct sun and keep well-watered. In winter the shoot will die down. Keep the rhizome dry until new growth appears the following spring.

plants
OF THE
month
2

HERBS FOR THE
CONSERVATORY

SHISO
(Perilla frutescens)

This bushy annual is widely grown in eastern Asia as a herb for culinary use. In Japan, the leaves are used in bean curd stir fries, tempura and pickles. The purple-leaved variety is used as an ornamental plant in summer bedding schemes.

category	Easy
type	Annual
flowers	Spikes of modest white flowers
leaves	Ovate, deeply-veined leaves with a strong, aromatic scent
height	60cm–1.2m (2–4ft)
spread	30–60cm (12–24in)
temperature	Frost free
position	Sun or partial shade
planting	20cm (8in) plastic or glazed pots to retain moisture

compost	Rich, moisture retentive, such as JI No. 3 or peat-based all-purpose compost
care	Pinch out outgrowing tips to make plant bushy. Keep well watered
propagation	Sow seed in early spring
species and	The frilled purple-leaved variety is *P. f.* 'Crispa' and has pink or red flower spikes

FRENCH PARSLEY
(Petroselinum crispum 'Neapolitanum'*)*

Fresh parsley is one of the most useful herbs to grow, both for its flavour and its decorative uses. The French (or often, Italian) parsley is more strongly flavoured than the curled variety but is not as hardy and so benefits from the shelter of the conservatory.

category	Easy
type	Hardy biennial

flowers	Small, greenish yellow heads
leaves	Rich green, flat and deeply cut
height	30cm (12in). Flowering stalks can reach 60cm (24in)
spread	30cm (12in)
temperature	Frost free
position	Good light
planting	Transplant into a special parsley pot or singly into 12cm (5in) pots
compost	Rich, moisture retentive, such as JI No. 3 or peat-based all-purpose compost
care	Keep well watered. Flowering shoots can be removed
propagation	Soak seeds in hot water and sow from early spring to early summer or in autumn in seed compost Parsley is slow to germinate and needs to be kept at a temperature of 21–27°C (70–80°F) for up to three weeks. Transplant as soon as large enough to handle
species and varieties	*P. c.* 'Moss curled', is the familiar tightly curled variety and it also grows well in pots

BASIL
(Ocimum basilicum)

Basil is the perfect accompaniment for tomatoes and although tomatoes are available all year, they do lose their flavour in winter. The answer is to grow a pot of basil in the conservatory. Cultivars are available with striking purple-black leaves, or with curled and ruffled foliage and are especially decorative.

category	Easy
type	Half hardy annual
flowers	White racemes of small flowers at the end of the stems
leaves	Bright green, oval, up to 5cm (2in) long
height	20–60cm (6–18in)
spread	15–45cm (24in)
temperature	10–15°C (50–59°F)
position	Full sun
planting	12cm (5in) pots
compost	JI No. 2 with added sand or grit for good drainage
care	Pinch out growing tips to encourage a bushy habit

propagation	Seed sown in spring at a temperature of 13–21°C (55–70°F)
species and varieties	*O. b.* 'Dark Opal' has purple-black leaves and cerise pink flowers. *O. b.* 'Purple Ruffles' has purple black leaves that are large, fringed and crinkly. *O. b.* var. *citriodorum* has narrow leaves with a scent of lemon. It is used in Indoesian cooking. If you can find it, *O. b.* 'Mini Purpurascens Wellsweep' forms a compact mound of purple flushed leaves 15–21cm (6–8in) high and 24–30cm (10–12in) across. *O. b.* 'Genovese' is the large-leaved variety seen in supermarkets

CHILLI PEPPER
(*Capsicum annuum* var. *annuum*)

These small, fiery relations of the bell pepper make wonderfully ornamental pot plants. More cultivars are becoming available and can be obtained with long narrow, or round fruits, upright or drooping, in pale yellow – which ripens to bright red – orange, purple or dark green. Their pungency ranges from mild to very hot

category	Easy
type	Tender annual
flowers	Small potato flowers in white or yellow
leaves	Oval-lance-shaped
height	45cm–1m (18in–3ft)
spread	60cm (24in)
temperature	18–21°C (64–70°F)
position	Full sun
planting	25cm (10in) pots
compost	JI No. 2 or all-purpose compost
care	Keep well watered and examine regularly for pests. Whitefly, aphid and red spider mite can be a problem
propagation	Sow seed in early spring
species and varieties	*C. a.* var. *a.* 'Anaheim' is mildly pungent and fruits can be 20cm (8in) long. *C. a.* var. *a.* 'Chili Serrano' is prolific, extremely hot and has shorter (8cm/3in) fruits. *C. a.* var. *a.* 'Super Cayenne' has very slender, hot fruits. *C. annuum*, bell pepper, is also worth trying

DECEMBER

As the year moves on, temperatures begin to fall consistently low.
Wonderful things are beginning to happen in the conservatory yet this
is a time when the excitement of Christmas intervenes, when it is
almost too easy to neglect the conservatory, to forget to water the bulbs
and overwintering seedlings, to ventilate and provide the movement
of air that prevents the growth of fungal diseases or the secret build-up
of pests.

Abutilon megapotamicum *is still flowering, the red and yellow
lanterns hanging like Christmas decorations from the arching canes,
seemingly unfazed by frost outside or the greyest of days. Azaleas are a
mass of bloom while there are fat buds on camellias and narrower
ones on* Jasminum polyanthemum *winding its way overhead. Pots of
bulbs are thickets of exciting shoots. Citrus blossom is perfuming the
air but although last month's stars may still be on stage, next month's
daphne and acacia will be waiting in the wings. In the conservatory,
as in the garden, one can never be too certain about what will happen.
Quality of light, as well as temperature, can speed up or retard
flowering to a surprising extent.*

Add extra colour by moving pot plants in. Many will flourish in the
conservatory if kept in a shaded place, perhaps in the lee of a larger
plant. Cyclamen in particular enjoy the moister, cooler atmosphere
and will reward you by flowering for much longer. Their colours blend
well with that of Indian azaleas and may continue for several weeks
to complement early-flowering camellias.

tasks
FOR THE
month

CLEANING THE CONSERVATORY

If the conservatory has not been thoroughly cleaned, now is the last time to do it. Choose a mild day. Tender plants can go inside the house, while others can have an airing outdoors for a few hours in the middle of the day. Do not overlook the roof – inside or out! Clean glass is particularly important throughout the winter because light levels are low and the days short

PRUNING ROSES

Prune roses in pots by removing weak or dead branches and cutting back others to an outward-facing bud.

PRUNING VINES

Prune grape vines (see p.102 for method).

PREPARED BULBS

Specially 'prepared' bulbs that were bought in late summer or early autumn will have shoots of 2.5–5cm (1–2in) by now. They should be brought into a shady, cool but frost-free place at the very beginning of the month.

■ A week later move the pot to a lighter position, then into the sunniest spot available. Soon the flower buds will appear.

■ Keep the pots well watered. Hyacinths, which have very heavy flowering spikes, and the taller narcissi, will need supporting.

■ After the flowers have died, cut the heads off, but leave as much stem as possible.

■ Keep watering and feeding until the leaves turn yellow.
■ Allow the bulbs to dry off and then store in a cool, dry place until next year.

■ The bulbs cannot be 'forced' again, but can be planted in the garden or repotted to flower a week or two earlier than they would normally in the garden.

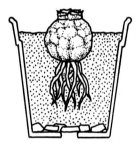

Hippeastrums
If you have a prepared hippeastrum hybrid like 'Appleblossom', it should have the roots soaked in lukewarm water for a few days before planting and the pots used must be 8cm (3in) in diameter larger than the bulbs. Use JI No. 3 compost and plant hippeastrums with half the bulb showing above the soil surface. The top half of the bulb should not be covered by compost (see above).

Hyacinths
Pots of prepared hyacinths almost in bloom are widely available at this time of year. Buy some for the house – if you have not bought bulbs and planted them yourself earlier – and buy one or two extra pots to fill the conservatory with perfume later.

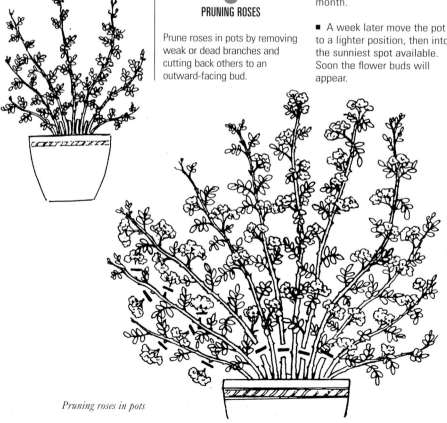

Pruning roses in pots

ROUTINE TASKS

Continue to ventilate the conservatory on bright, warm days

Sterilize pots and trays in a disinfectant solution. Wear rubber gloves

Inspect the plants regularly, checking for pests and removing dead leaves and spent flowers

Whitefly can be troublesome. If sticky traps have not made much impact, fumigate or spray

Fuchsias, heliotropes and other plants being dried off and overwintered out of sight should be checked. Make sure that there are no dead leaves left on the pots where pests could hide

Kumquats are in shops now. They make good pot plants (as well as preserves) although they are slow growing. Buy some extra fruit and sow the pips straight away. They need a temperature of between 16–21°C (61–70°F) to germinate

Check spring-flowering bulbs that have been left in a cool place

Do some reading. And planning. Remember, the conservatory changes as the garden does. Some plants will grow larger and cut out light (or provide patches of welcome shade for different types of plant)

Palms, aspidistras and dracaenas will benefit from a wash with tepid water into which a few drops of milk have been stirred

---

WATERING

If using water from a water-butt outside (recommended for plants like citrus, azalea and camellias that must have soft water), fill the watering can and let it stand in the conservatory for several hours to warm up. If you do not have a water-butt, leave a bucket outside to collect rainwater or get into the habit of saving any water remaining in the kettle after it has been boiled.

In an unheated conservatory most plants need to be watered very sparingly during the winter. Once a fortnight may be enough. Water carefully to avoid splashing the leaves or crowns of the plants. To prevent water from rotting the corms of cyclamen, it is best to water the plants from below by standing the pot in a saucer of water. As soon as the compost at the top has darkened, remove the pot from the saucer and let it drain. Do this in the morning.

Plants in a heated conservatory will still need some humidity in the atmosphere, even in winter. Group the plants that are in flower on shallow trays filled with gravel or clay pellets. Add sufficient water to keep the gravel wet. Make sure though that the bottoms of the pots are not sitting in the water as this

can cause the roots to rot.

If a plant is showing signs of overwatering (see p.46) and on inspection, proves to have waterlogged soil, it may be possible to revive it.
- Remove the plant from the pot. If you have difficulty removing it and it is in a small plastic pot, hold the plant carefully, tip the pot upside down and give the rim a sharp tap on a hard surface.

- A large plant in a terracotta pot can be extracted by first running a knife or the long blade of a pruning saw round the inside.

- Then place the pot on its side and gently tap it all round with a piece of wood. This should loosen the compost.

- Remove the soggy compost from the roots and then snip off any rotting roots and leaves.

- Repot in fresh compost.

Plants in dried out compost should be immersed in a bucket of water for an hour or so, until bubbles stop rising. Use rainwater if the plants dislike lime. Both rainwater and tap water should be tepid. This immersion should be carried out early in the day and the plant allowed to drain well afterwards.

---

plants

OF THE

month

 ## LEMON TREE
(Citrus × meyeri 'Meyer')

The very first conservatories were orangeries which were built to house citrus trees in the sixteenth century. All citruses have glossy evergreen leaves, fragrant flowers over a long period, and fruit too. Many flower and fruit at the same time, making a very attractive impression. *C.* × *m.* 'Meyer' is easy to grow and flowers throughout the year. It produces pale, juicy fruit.

category	Fragrant
type	Evergreen tree/shrub
flowers	Five waxy white petals flushed with pinky-purple underneath
leaves	Long, oval, green, glossy
height	1.8m (6ft)
spread	1.2m (4ft)
temperature	10°C (50°F)
position	Full sun
planting	20–25cm (8–10in) pots or small tubs during the winter. Citrus dislike root disturbance
compost	JI No. 2
care	Water plants with tepid rainwater. Keep just moist in winter. Water more freely in summer. Spray the leaves daily in hot weather and keep the conservatory well ventilated. Only repot in winter, or top dress with a 5cm (2in) layer of JI No. 3. Citrus dislike sudden changes in temperature and humidity. They can be put outside during the summer if necessary but prefer to stay in one place. (See also p.103)
propagation	Take 8–10cm (3–4in) long semi-ripe cuttings during summer and root in a propagator at a temperature of 16–18°C (61–64°F). When rooted, prick out into 8cm (3in) pots of JI No. 2. For propagation from seed, see p.76
species and varieties	*C. aurantiifolia* × *limon* 'Indian Lime is prickly, but very fruitful and the fruit has a good lime flavour; the Calamondin orange, X *Citrofortunella* is a very decorative dwarf bush, with small fruits, intermediate between a kumquat and an orange; *C. sinensis* is the sweet orange and there are many good varieties including *C. s.* 'Washington' from California and *C. s.* 'Valencia'

 ## INDOOR AZALEAS
(Rhododendron simsii cultivars)

The Indian azalea, with small evergreen leaves, is covered with flowers ranging in colour from rose-pink to dark red, for many weeks. Cultivars are also available with salmon-pink, white and orange flowers. An unheated but frost-free conservatory suits these widely available pot plants very well. Buy a plant of the shade you like with lots of buds and just one or two flowers already open.

category	Easy
type	Evergreen shrub
flowers	Widely funnel-shaped, sometimes double, 5cm (2in) across, in clusters at the end of the branches
leaves	Neat, leathery, dark green, narrowly oval
height	To 1.5m (5ft) but much less in pots
spread	To 1.5m (5ft) but less in pots
temperature	3–7°C (37–45°F)
position	Good light
planting	In autumn in a 15–25cm (6–10in) pot according to size of plant
compost	Ericaceous compost
care	Keep plants moist at all times, using rainwater or boiled, cooled water. Do not let the compost dry out at all but particularly in summer when the plant will be forming flower buds for the following winter. Keep the plants outdoors until midwinter and bring inside for flowering. Maintain a humid atmosphere. When there is no

possibility of further frosts, stand outside again in a cool, shady place for the summer. Feed with a fertilizer formulated for acid-loving plants while the plant is in growth. Repot in spring if necessary. Azaleas are reputed to flower better if pot-bound

propagation	Take 5–8cm (2–3in) long semi-ripe cuttings in summer and root them in a mixture of peat and sand or a lime-free cutting compost at a temperature of 16°C (61°F). They are difficult to root but more successful if treated with hormone rooting powder or gel and placed in a mist propagator
species and varieties	Other tender rhododendrons that flourish in a cool conservatory are *R.* 'Fragrantissimum', white flowers tinged pink, *R.* 'Lady Alice Fitzwilliam', white flowers stained yellow and *R.* 'Countess of Haddington', pink flowers

COLUMNEA
(*Columnea* × *banksii*)

When in full bloom, this plant is a waterfall of vivid scarlet. The showy, hooded flowers appear from every leaf axil. Plant trailing columneas where the long stems can be allowed to hang down to their fullest extent.

category	Challenging
type	Semi-trailing epiphyte
flowers	Bright red, tubular, hooded to 8cm (3in) long, along the stem
leaves	Small, oval, thick and glossy
height	90cm (3ft)
spread	Indefinite
temperature	Minimum of 10°C (50°F) but maintain 13–16°C (55–61°F) for continuous flowering
position	Bright position but out of full sun
planting	25cm (10in) hanging pot or basket
compost	Peat-based compost or two parts JI No. 2 to one part sphagnum moss
care	In summer, ventilate the conservatory well when temperature is above 18°C (64°F). Shade the glass and water freely. Maintain a humid atmosphere. In winter, keep plants just moist. Re-pot in alternate years in summer. Give a weak liquid feed every week from late spring to early autumn
propagation	Take 8cm (3in) long cuttings from non-flowering stems in early to late spring. Insert in a mixture of sand and peat or proprietary cutting compost. Root in a propagator at a temperature of 18–21°C (64–70°F). When rooted, pot up into 8cm (3in) pots of the growing compost. Pinch out tips to ensure a bushy habit. Three young plants can be planted up in a hanging basket
species and varieties	*C.* 'Broget Stavanger' has very small, variegated leaves. *C. schiedeana* is easy, fast growing and tolerant of lower temperatures. *C.* 'Merkur' has bright yellow flowers

IVY
(*Hedera canariensis* 'Gloire de Marengo')

The bold leaves of *H. c.* 'Gloire de Marengo' look good all year round and will thrive in a north-facing conservatory provided there is sufficient light.

category	Cool and shady
type	Evergreen climber
flowers	When mature, drumstick heads of small whitish-green flowers followed by black berries
leaves	Large, triangular, with reddish-purple stems and silver variegation
height	6m (20ft) after many years
spread	5m (16½ft)
temperature	3–7°C (37–45°F)
position	Good light and some shade
planting	10–15cm (4–6in) pots
compost	JI No. 2
care	If atmosphere gets too dry, mist well. Water normally. Give a liquid feed occasionally during summer
propagation	10cm (4in) long cuttings should root in water. (See p.88.) To propagate an ivy bush rather than a climber, take the cuttings from adult growth (see p.69)
species and varieties	*H. helix* 'Buttercup', is is slow growing with yellow leaves; *H. helix* 'Parsley Crested' has frilly edges to the leaves. *H. helix* 'Tricolor' is grey-green, silver-edged and flushes pink in winter

practical
project

MAKING A HEATED
PROPAGATOR

There are many thermostatically controlled propagators available, in a range of sizes from those small enough to fit on to a window-sill to others which will take several full-size seed trays. Making your own propagators, however, using heated cables in moist sand, allows more freedom in the shape and height of the propagator. You can construct it to fit the available space and make it tall enough to be used for overwintering a variety of tender plants.

Cables are available in four sizes:

- 50 watts, 3.05m (10ft) long to heat 0.45sq m (4–5sq ft)

- 75 watts, 6.1m (20ft) for an area of 0.85sq m (8–10sq ft)

- 150 watts, 12.2m (40ft) long suitable for 1.7sq m (16–20sq ft)

- 300 watts, 24.4m (80ft) long for an area of 3.85sq m (36–40sq ft)

7.5 watts per 30cm (12in) square of bench will raise the soil temperature by approximately 10–15°C (20–25°F).

YOU WILL NEED

A frame made of:
- *Wooden boards, 18–23cm (7–9in) wide and 1.5cm (⁵/₈in) thick*
- *Base of wood or marine-quality plywood (If this is to stand on a bench, the frame will not need a base. However, if it is to rest on a slightly smaller table or other form of support, a sturdy base is necessary)*
A soil warming cable
A horticultural thermostat
A three-pin plug fitted with a 5 amp fuse
Screwdriver (electrical is best)
Electric drill and 8mm drill bit
Screws (or hammer and nails)
Polythene or roofing felt
Rigid polystyrene insulation at least 2.5cm (1in) thick
Coarse sand

Making the frame
- Make up the frame to the selected dimensions.

- Drill two holes in the side of the frame. One is to take the soil warming cable which is in three parts – the yellow warming cable, which must *not* be altered in any way; a black mains lead which can be shortened if necessary, and a seal between the two. This can be outside or inside the frame. The other hole is to take the thermostat rod.

- Line it with polythene or roofing felt and then cover the base with the rigid polystyrene insulation.

- Cover this with a 5cm (2in) deep layer of sand.

Laying the heating cable
- Lay the yellow heating cable evenly over the surface as shown in the diagram.

- Avoid sharp bends.

- Do **not** allow the cable to cross itself at any point because this will make it overheat and burn out.

- For the same reason it is important that you do not lay the cable so that the lengths are less than 5cm (2in) apart.
- If the cable does not bend easily, it should be fully extended and connected to the electricity supply and switched on for a very short time. It will then become more flexible.

- The aluminium rod of the thermostat should be placed just above the cable. For wiring the thermostat plate and the lead from the soil warming cable, follow the instructions given by the manufacturers.

- Cover the soil cable and thermostat rod with a further 5cm (2in) deep layer of coarse sand. The sand must then be watered and kept permanently moist to ensure even heat distribution. Failure to do this will cause the cable to burn out.

MAKING A PROPAGATOR COVER

The simplest way of using the sand bench to overwinter plants is to insert a cane into each corner and drape it with horticultural fleece or bubble polythene. Alternatively, the propagator can be constructed to the size of a

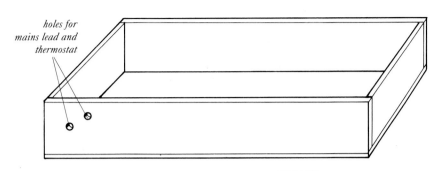

holes for mains lead and thermostat

SIMPLE WOODEN FRAME WITH BASE

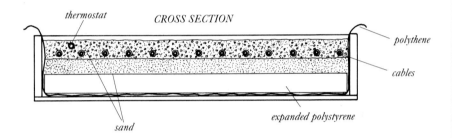

thermostat *CROSS SECTION*

polythene

cables

sand *expanded polystyrene*

CABLE ARANGEMENT

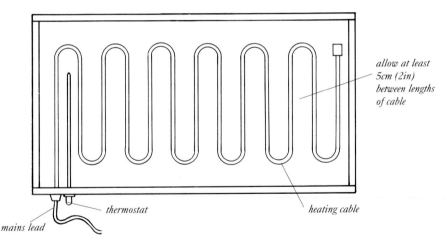

allow at least 5cm (2in) between lengths of cable

thermostat *heating cable*

mains lead

commercially available cloche. The most effective are those with walls of structured polycarbonate. For small plants, the cloister cloche is easy to handle and has a hinged panel for easy access. Also available are decorative Victorian-style cloches which are 56cm (22in) high in the centre and have a removable top. These are very attractive for a period conservatory, but rather expensive.

An experienced woodworker could make a simple but more permanent framework for a propagator cover by cutting four battens 47 x 15mm (1⁷/₈ x ⁵/₈in) softwood to the length necessary.

■ Make a bird's mouth joint (see p.92) at the lower end and a mitre at the top end. Join the mitred ends, making two right angle pieces.

■ Glue and pin one to each end of the basic frame and join the two ends across the top with 2.5 x 2.5cm (1 x 1in) aluminium or standard wooden corner moulding. This does not have to carry any weight so can be quite flimsy.

USEFUL ADDRESSES

CONSERVATORIES AND GLASSHOUSES TO VISIT

The Temperate House at the Royal Botanic Gardens, Kew

The Glasshouses at the Royal Horticultural Society's Garden at Wisley, Surrey

Bicton Park, East Budleigh, Budleigh Salterton, Devon

Glasgow University Botanic Garden

West Dean College, West Sussex has a wonderful collection of Victorian glasshouses

Belfast Botanic Gardens has a palm house and tropical ravine

National Botanic Garden, Glasnevin, Dublin has a range of recently restored glasshouses

FERTILIZERS AND PEST CONTROL

Garden Direct
Geddings Road
Hoddesdon, Herts. EN11 0LR
Tel: 01992 441888

(Mail order pesticides, fertilizers, hormone rooting powder, etc)

EQUIPMENT

Two Wests & Elliott Ltd
Unit 4, Carrwood Road
Sheepbridge Industrial Estate
Chesterfield
Derbyshire S41 9RH
Tel: 01246 4541077

The Traditional Garden Supply Company
Unit 12, Hewitts Industrial Estate
Elmbridge Road
Cranleigh, Surrey GU6 8LW
Tel: 01483 273366

Mastermind Products Ltd
Porter's Lodge
Bowerwood Road
Fordingbridge
Hampshire SP6 2BS
Tel: 01425 656942

(Watermate: pumped automatic watering system utilizing rainwater from a butt)

PLANTS

P. & S. Allanson
Rhendhoo
Jurby
Isle of Man IM7 3HB
Tel: 01624 880766

(Specialize in plants from Australia and New Zealand)

Jacques Amand
The Nurseries
Clamp Hill
Stanmore
Middlesex HA7 3JS
Tel: 0181 954 8138

(Tender bulbs and bulbous plants)

Architectural Plants
Cooks Farm
Nuthurst
Horsham
West Sussex RH13
Tel: 01403 891772

Avon Bulbs
Burnt House Farm
Mid Lambrook
South Petherton
Somerset TA13 5HE
Tel: 01460 242177

(Wide range of bulbs)

Bridgmere Garden World
Bridgemere
Nantwich
Cheshire CW5 7QB
Tel: 01270 520381/520239

(Wide collection of tropical foliage plants and many others)

Broadleigh Gardens
Bishops Hull
Taunton
Somerset TA4 1AE
Tel: 01823 286231

(Small bulbs especially species narcissus)

Burncoose & South Down Nurseries
Gwennap
Redruth
Cornwall TR16 6BJ
Tel: 01209 861112

(Wide range of conservatory plants)

Dibley's Nurseries
Llanelidan
Ruthin, Clwyd LL15 2LG
Tel: 01978 790677

(Specialize in streptocarpus, begonias, coleus
(solenostemon) and other gesneriads)

Fibrex Nurseries Ltd
Honeyburne Road
Pebworth
Stratford Upon Avon CV37 8XT
Tel: 01789 720788

(Ivies, ferns, pelargoniums)

Greenholm Nurseries
Lampley Road
Kingston Seymour
Clevedon
Avon BS21 6XS
Tel: 01943 83350

(Passion flowers)

Heather & Brian Hiley
25 Little Woodcote Estate
Wallington
Surrey SM5 4AU
Tel: 0181 647 9679

(Tender and unusual plants)

McBeans Orchids
Cooksbridge
Lewes
East Sussex BN8 4PR
Tel: 01273 400228

Reads Nursery
Hales Hall
Loddon
Norfolk NR14 6QW
Tel: 01508 548395

(Wide range of conservatory plants, citrus
fruits, grape vines and figs, including large
specimens)

Clive Simms
Woodhurst
Essendine
Stamford
Lincolnshire PE9 4LQ
Tel: 01780 55615

(Unusual fruiting plants)

Stapeley Water Gardens
London Road
Stapeley, Nantwich
Cheshire CW5 7LH
Tel: 01270 623868

(Aquatic plants)

Toobees Exotics
20 Inglewood
Woking
Surrey GU21 3HX
Tel: 01483 722600

(Rare and unusual succulents)

Tropical Rainforest
66 Castle Grove Avenue
Leeds LS6 4BS
Tel: 0113 2789810

(Bromeliads)

The Vernon Geranium Nursery
Cuddington Way
Cheam, Sutton
Surrey SM2 7JB
Tel: 0181 393 7616

Westdale Nurseries
Holt Road
Bradford-on-Avon
Wilts BA15 1TS
Tel: 0122 586 3258

(Bougainvilleas)

FURTHER READING

The RHS Plant Finder. (Any current edition is an indispensable guide to finding specialist plant suppliers)

RHS Gardeners' Encyclopedia of Plants and Flowers Dorling Kindersley, London

Glasshouses May Woods and Arete Warren, Aurum Press, London

The Conservatory Gardener Anne Swithinbank, Frances Lincoln, London

The Complete Guide to Conservatory Plants Ann Bonar, Collins & Brown, London

The Greenhouse Expert Dr D. G. Hessayon, Expert Books, London

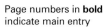 # INDEX